Quality Customer Service

Sharon L. Burton, MBA

Quality Customer Service

Rekindling the Art of Service to Customers

Second Edition

Lulu Publications

This publication is designed to provide competent and reliable information regarding the subject matter.

Although based on true cases, certain locations, and names have been fictionalized for educational content and impact.

Lulu Publications
Second Edition

A wide variety of references are listed. Reasonable efforts were made to publish reliable information, but the author and publisher cannot assume responsibility for the validity of all materials or for the consequences of their use.

Second Edition

ISBN-13   978-0-6151-4897-7

This book was published on-demand in cooperation with Lulu Publishing. On-demand publishing is a distinctive process and service of making a book available for retail sale to the public taking advantage of on-demand manufacturing and Internet marketing. On-demand publishing includes promotions. Retail sales, manufacturing, order fulfillment, accounting and collecting royalties on behalf of the author.

Cover design by William E. Smith, Ph.D.

Quote

Visualize this thing that you want. See it, feel it, believe in it.
Make your mental blueprint, and begin to build!

Robert Collier

(PPP Retirement Plans, (n.d.). "Creative Visualization...")

PREFACE

Quality customer service is the major component of any customer seeking business. Customers remain loyal to businesses paying attention to the details of customer service. One of the main reason businesses fail is due to a consistent decline in their attention surrounding the art of service to customers.

In Albany, Georgia, during my years at Dougherty Jr. High School, I had the opportunity to have great teachers who initially instilled within me the desire to write. I studied different writing styles, then began to write articles for the school's newspaper, poetry, short stories, and etc.

I pursued a BS degree in Criminology, completed an internship at the regional crime lab in Albany, Georgia, and thought I would pursue a career in crime scene investigation, plus training. The training bug continued to fester. My career switched gears. I worked in customer service and human resources arenas while observing human behaviors and patterns. The word customer took on a new definition for me, for I focused on the internal, as well as the external customer.

In addition to studying customer service in the work place, I studied other businesses. Jotting notes of great customer service and poor customer service became a ritual. When experiencing great or poor customer service, I took the process further by asking for a manager or person in charge. While explaining the situation, I paid attention to the different responses. Continued studies have led to the book and seminar series, *Quality Customer Service Rekindling the Art of Service to Customers.*

This easy to read book details customer service as told through the experiences of seven friends. These friends conduct a customer service brainstorming session, then decide to seek customer service in different businesses. The characters are Dollar, Stu, Meaty, Shopper, Peachie, Medic, and BATS.

In this story each character is faced with a plethora of customer service events. The seven characters represent different varieties of businesses. At the end of the week long journey, the friends reunite to discuss their experiences with customer service plus the skills they increased and learned. The group leader, BATS, delivers insight on dealing with and exhibiting great internal and external customer service.

Whether your career is in the financial industry, education, grocery business, retail industry, restaurant business, medical field, transportation industry, or any other field, *Quality Customer Service Rekindling the Art of Service to Customers* is an accounting of the art of service to customer to be read by all. Readers will gain an increased understanding of the importance of customer service. Moreover the book shows how a dedicated customer service program must flow from the top down with measurable deliverables.

ACKNOWLEDGEMENTS

My mentors have said customer service is very important; without consistent and quality service there are no customers. The completion of this book is a compilation of experiences, study, research, and commitment. I want to thank the English teachers who touched my life and developed me into a writer. I thank Chuck Helmer, a mentor, who inspired me to continue my dream of excelling in the field of training and development, and Thomas Harmon for allowing me the latitude of my skills. Evagelos Ekkizogloy, thank you for your words of encouragement.

I thank my fore parents, Agnes Hill Williams, Henry Williams, Ellen Flakes Burton, and Zelmo Burton, for life. I thank my relatives, Synster Johnson, Marvin Hill, and Soloman Jones, Sr. who aided me in a crucial time of life. There is much love for my family Roosevelt Burton, Mary Johnson, Lucile Jones, Myrtle, Tekeela Regina, Jovetta, Duane, Paul, Roxanne, Theopulius, Wykesia, Marquies, Darrieus, and Myesha. I thank my long term extended families, the Smiths, Canon Edwin and Mrs. Alma Smith, Edwin Jr., Cynthia, Edwin III, Elizabeth, Alan, William, Don, Maria, Gabby, Don Jr., Eileen, Fred, Freddie, Stephanie, Cassie, Daniel, and Emmanuel, plus Rudolph & Nancy Oliver.

Janice and Warren, thank you for everything. Additional thanks goes out to Braxton & Connie Cabble, Donald & Deloris Green, Ozella Weaver, Michael Woodard, Vincent &Thelma Shedrick, Curtis Jones, Earl & Lorelei Green, Lydia Anderson, Vivian Williams, Diane Clarke-Streett, Teresa Mason, Edwin Holland, Nadine Blue-Smith, Patricia Smith-Walker, Linda Foltz, Kelley Robinson, Angela Washington, Stacy Allen, Patricia Purcell, Denise Nordheimer, Jeff Cooke, the Shuler Group, Gloria McCray, Ralin and Sharon Sanders, plus Guy & Shirley Anderson.

Special thanks to the people assisting in the construction of this work, William E. Smith, Ph.D., Francene Perry-Brown, Ed.D., Yoshino N. Woodard, MS, and Shirley Evans, BS.

Wilmington, DE, the city which provided me with a solid foundation to nurture my daughter, plus offers me my place of rest, I thank you too.

TABLE OF CONTENTS

LIST OF SERVICE REVIEW TABLES

LIST OF CHARTS

Quote

"Four things come not back - the spoken word, the sped arrow, the past life, and the neglected opportunity."

An Arabian Proverb

(Chambliss, Meisel, Wolf, 1991, "Light One Candle...," p. 25)

INTRODUCTION

One Sunday evening Dollar, Stu, Meaty, Shopper, Peachie, Medic, and BATS sat in the great room of their five bedrooms and five bathrooms home and discussed a host of topics. Focused on saving for the future, the seven of them decided to purchase a home together. After three hours of conversation, the topic of customer service surfaced. Dollar asked, "What is a customer?" Meaty replied, "One definition of a customer is an individual who buys goods or services."

Shopper replied, "A customer is the most important person a business can work with. The customer helps to keep the business prosperous."

"The customer is the most fundamental asset of a business," said Peachie.

"Great answers. Now let us put all of this information together and analyze it," said BATS. "What you all seem to be saying is, "The customer is a business' most valuable asset; because, the customer purchases goods and services the business works to provide for a profit."

"Great summation!," shouted Dollar, Stu, Meaty, Shopper, Peachie, and Medic.

"Now that we have determined the customer, let's discuss customer service," said BATS. "As we all may know, the type of service a customer receives is fundamental to the customer returning to a business whether it is online or a physical location. Why don't you tell us your understanding of customer service, Dollar?"

Dollar sat back in his chaise lounge and regarded his friends attentively for a few moments. He then raised his head and said, "I believe customer service is making the customer smile. What do you think Stu?"

Stu smiled and said, "Customer service is the conglomerate of actions a business embarks on during dealings with its customers."

Meaty stood and walked around for a few minutes, nodding as he usually does. "Great! I like what you all have said. Customer service is important within a business, as well. Different departments must treat each other with care. Department to department interaction is internal customer service." What about you Shopper?"

"Customer service is applicable to retail establishments, banks, educational institutions, grocery stores, restaurants, the transportation industry, the medical arena, as well as all other industries. Customer service should be the catalyst extending to repeat business and referrals."

Peachie laughed, as always entertained by her friends' lively conversations.

"Well I guess it is my turn. Customer service, to some is to get a low price. On the other hand customer service is timely delivery, great service, strong support, and a representative able to work with all types of customers." She continued, "I have seen where customer service delivers generational differences. These variations influence expectations in regards to delivery of service. In order for each generation level to reach the others, training and development is definitely the key to ensuring that all customers' needs are met"

Chart 1: Quality Customer Service and the Generations

Quality Customer Service and the Generations		
1979-1995	Generation Y (Millennials)	Any Generation Y environment should be flexible. There has to be numerous opportunities for growth and teamwork. This group has plenty of self esteem. They believe in structure and the use of technology.
1965-1978	Generation X	This group grew-up watching television and are very media savvy. Births were below the national average. This group does not have the belief in control as do the baby boomers. It craves less order than the baby boomers. This group focuses on self needs. They are comfortable with technology.
1945-1964	Baby Boomers	This group will fight for a cause, and have a belief in government control. Process and order are key words for this group. The later boomers may be more comfortable with technology than the earlier boomers.
X -1944	Matures	This group was born before 1945 and is very methodical. This group is slow to change. This group shies away from the use of technology as tools to learn through.

Peachie continued, "Businesses should be aware of the different generations' responses to education and training. When teaching customer service techniques educators must be aware of the learning styles. Overall general learning styles have a direct relationship to the generations. These diverse generations will process and relay information differently.

Generation Xers up through the Millennials will more than likely have no fears about learning and teaching through the use of technology. The Matures, as well as the majority of the baby boomers, will choose a mode other than the computer from which to learn and teach.

Management should ensure that each generation learns the skills necessary to support the wide customer bases that are possibly made up of all the generations."

"Great job," remarked BATS.

Full of life, passionate, and expressive, BATS maintains an outgoing and friendly persona. Fairly known for taking control, BATS enjoys being in charge. Even so, he is forthcoming, generous, and approachable.

"Now it is my turn," he said. "According to all of you, customer service is the ability or skill to service a customer with a smile. Moreover, customer service is timely delivery, great service, strong support, a representative able to work with all types of customers, and the catalyst extending to repeat business and referrals. I have an idea. Each of you should go out and seek customer service one day this week. At the end of the week we will discuss each person's findings. If we gather enough information, we may be able to prepare a workshop, or even a series of workshops.

It appears as though many businesses and institutions of higher learning have succumbed to apathy. Boardrooms and conference rooms are filled with all levels of management talking about customer service, discussing seminars, and signing themselves and their employees up for courses. Beyond the talking and writing stages little else is done to fully execute deliverables designed to produce efficiency and effectiveness. There is no consistent plan of action."

Dollar, Stu, Meaty, Shopper, Peachie, Medic, and BATS, all excited about customer service, sat and pondered their next moves. Each knew he or she had to develop an individual plan to flush out the question of where is customer service. Numerous ideas rolled through their minds. Will I really find customer service? Where should I look for customer service? Who will be the most likely person to demonstrate customer service at the selected location? Will I know great customer service when I experience it? What type of customer service do customers want to receive from businesses and institutions?

The time was 8:30 PM, and no business would be open before 9:00 AM the next morning. BATS decided to sit and think more about the customer service venture. BATS, sitting in his favorite room, cozily decorated in mango and orange drifted into a peaceful thought process. He stood, poured a full mug of his favorite tea, and closed the door out of habit. BATS then sat back onto his massage lounger, listened to jazz by The W.E.S. Group, and pondered even more while the massage nodes moved up and down from his head to his toes.

A loud gurgle arose from BATS' stomach. He arched forward knowing he should have eaten long before now. The customer service conversation was so exciting he did not think about eating. Sitting in the massage chair was peaceful and quiet.

BATS thought, "I should have turned on the tape player." He frequently sat in his favorite chair and recorded his thoughts. He leaned over to the small intricately tile woven table of orange, mango, navy blue, and red, and pressed the record button on the miniature recorder.

"Customer service, in many cases, is departmentalized. Organizations separate representatives as to the category of customers handled. For example, a college may have different representatives serving students registering, students receiving financial aid, and students requiring certifications, and transcripts. A bank might have different departments servicing personal banking customers, and business banking customers." BATS' mind was on a roll.

What we really need to do is conduct a survey on customer service. The survey will supply data to help determine deficiencies and/or strengths in customer service. What is more, we will receive ideas that may help us focus on and develop key strategies for customer service. We just may uncover significant information on loyalty and satisfaction. I will be sure to share this survey idea with the team tomorrow."

BATS' thoughts centered entirely on the customer service project. Although the team thought he was sometimes too in-charge, BATS knew he was smart, swift, and on the ball. Even as a child, he had always been. And BATS was good at his position. His previous manager at Johnson Consulting told him he was great with brainstorming, and organizing think tanks. Because of his drive, determination, and talent he moved up the corporate ladder faster than most.

BATS, the planner of the team, turned off the recorder. Two minutes later he turned off the massage lounger, stood, then trotted through the great room to get some food. In the kitchen he found his team of friends consuming pizza and soda.

Standing in front of the CD player, his eyes scanned the shelf of discs. BATS loved music and in particular, jazz. He immediately picked up the gang's favorite CD, The W.E.S. Group, put it into the CD player, and then selected *Timelessness as the selection* to hear first. Deciding pizza was too heavy to eat at this hour of the night, he went for the salad.

"Team I have come up with another idea to add to our customer service venture. We need to incorporate a survey. We all should pool together some ideas for the survey, and determine the metrics."

"Great idea BATS," said Medic. "We need to send out enough surveys to receive a minimum of 100 completed surveys to analyze. Further, we should have around 15 categories, and incorporate a combination of qualitative and quantitative scoring. This information can be used in seminars."

"Furthermore", said Medic, "We need to look at all of the aspects of customer service as we seek people employing the art of customer service. As we see poor examples, we need to think about what may or may not be the cause of the behavior."

Medic continued. "Lets keep in mind boiling frog syndrome," said BATS. The story goes if a frog is placed in a pot of cold water and the pot is placed on a fire and slowly heated, the frog will sit in the water as it heats up and then boil to death. The frog consistently adjusts to the changing of the heat of the water. On the other hand, if the water is first heated, then the frog is dropped in, the frog will leap out of the water.

Companies, and educational institutions may become vulnerable to the 'boiled frog phenomenon'. Management may either fail to monitor their business operations due to a lack of understanding, or due to negligence and greed. This behavior may start small then escalate over time. Boiled frog syndrome can represent complacency in one of its worst forms. This syndrome has been intertwined into the greater scheme of the world since the beginning of time. No matter what the circumstance, suffering is the end result.

Internal and external customers must be able to see and experience enhanced customer service. Businesses must remain focused on the art of service to customers. It cannot be a fad that is reviewed one season and forgotten the next. Customer service must be a consistent mega movement. Management must ensure customer service is taught and shared in every department, at every level, and with every new hire."

"Medic, tell us more details of this boil frog phenomenon," said BATS.

Medic proceeded to speak. "Our culture is an example of boiled frog syndrome. Paraphrasing Radenau Schauspielhaus Wahnfried our culture glided into a pot of warm water approximately 20 thousand years ago when we learned totalitarian agriculture. "Totalitarian agriculture is based on the premise that all the food in the world belongs to us, and there is no limit whatsoever to what we may take for ourselves and deny to all others"(Radenau, S. W., (May 18), "The Boiling Frog"). Between 5000-3000 B.C.E. our culture became crowded and the land was worked excessively. The people were competing for fewer resources. During this time "...we see the first states formed for the purpose of armed defense and aggression" (Radenau, S. W., (May 18), "The Boiling Frog: Signs of Distress: 5000-3000 B.C.E."). Between 3000-1400 B.C.E., "crime was emerging" (Radenau, S. W., (May 18), "The Boiling Frog: Signs of Distress: 3000-1400 B.C.E."). Due to the mentality of our culture heating in the pot, "crime would join war as a measure of how hot the water was becoming around our smiling frog" (Radenau,

S. W., (May 18), "The Boiling Frog: Signs of Distress: 3000-1400 B.C.E."). Between 1400 and 0 B.C.E. "was an era of civil revolt and assassination" (Radenau, S. W., (May 18), "The Boiling Frog: Signs of Distress: 1400-0 B.C.E."), plus religion. These are more signs of the continued boiling. The period 0 and 1200 C.E. brought on an intense focus towards religion and salvation. Between 1200 and 1700 ghettos emerged, disease erupted, and excessive death raised it head. The pot continued to boil. Between 1700 and 1900 "mental illness...flourished, and economic instability remained high" (Radenau, S. W., (May 18), "The Boiling Frog: Signs of Distress: 1700-1900"). Between 1900 and 1960 our culture saw its "first global collapse, beginning 1929, [and] ...two cataclysmic world wars..." (Radenau, S. W., (May 18), "The Boiling Frog: Signs of Distress: 1900-60"). Between 1960 and 1996 we saw as "a social fixture war, crime, corruption, slavery, revolt, famine, plague, and drugs" (Radenau, S. W., (May 18), "The Boiling Frog: Signs of Distress: 1960-96"). From 1960 to the present time, we are experiencing "cultural collapse" (Radenau, S. W., (May 18), "The Boiling Frog: Signs of Distress: 1960-96"). The frog, our culture, has not only gradually heated, but is comfortable in this condition of decreased communication with others, ignorance, and turning a blind eye to issues and concerns.

Medic continued, "Again, as we seek out customer service this week, let us pay attention to signs of the customer service boiling frog. When did service start to decline. Note the incidents, then send BATS an email so he can prepare the presentation and lead the discussion on Sunday."

"Let me interject," said BATS. "Businesses should place an increased focus on establishing and employing an universal set of competencies for customer service. Such competencies should be taught in secondary and post secondary institutions, also. Customer service education delivers value through spawning insights and knowledge management systems. Such training offers a deeper understanding of customer dynamics. Strategically instituted quality customer service education, internal and external, will facilitate organizations in managing their human capital efforts more effectively. Management should evaluate the long-range impacts of different customer service strategies and use such information in creating customer service models to entice the target and niche markets.

As I think of standards, I am reminded that Dollar once worked in project management and user acceptance testing. He was trained in ISO 9000, which is a process standard applying to all business types. ISO 9000 is a quality standard that is prominent around the world. This standard is so popular because it controls quality, saves money, and has to account for customer satisfaction.

ISO is the International Organization for Standardization. International Organization for Standardization is a voluntary, non-treaty organization founded in 1946. It is responsible for establishing international standards in many areas, to include computers and communications. ISO 9000 was "first established in 1987" and "oriented towards compliance or what we have termed conformance quality" (Schroeder, 2004, Operations Management..., p. 143).

As ISO 9000 is for many businesses around the world, companies need to think of their employees' soft skills in a manner that consistently demands and delivers quality customer service."

As the friends sat and ate, their minds drifted with the melodious tones of *Timelessness*. This circle of friends had no idea they were in motion towards destiny. Nor did they know their lives were about to be transformed, and so intensely they would never be the same as before.

And later, when Dollar, Stu, Meaty, Shopper, Peachie, Medic, and BATS reflect back to this very night, they would look fascinated and reminiscent to themselves why they had not been cognizant something big was going to happen. At the time they had not comprehended they were about to set out on the search of their lives.

Questions

1. Why is the customer the most important person a business can work with?

2. What are the key ingredients for customer service?

3. Review boiled frog syndrome in relationship to
customer service?

4. How does customer service education delivers value?

Notes

Notes

Quote

"I will study and get ready and the opportunity will come."

Abraham Lincoln

(Chambliss, et al., (1991), p. 47)

Chapter 1

Dollar, Banking and Customer Service

Monday morning, Dollar packed his vehicle with his brief case, a lunch bag, and drove down Bentree Road until he reached the main road. The drive into the city would be hectic. Monday's traffic seemed to always be the worse. Since the opening of the Woodrow Wilson Bridge, maybe the pressure will be lifted off of Interstate 295. The early Maryland morning appeared hazy. The route Dollar decided to take from the house to the credit union is a familiar one. Dollar has been a member of the credit union for the past five years. This credit union was attached to Dollar's company. For the past five years he had money directly deposited into accounts at the credit union.

Dollar reached the credit union right at 9:00 AM. He walked into the spacious location of designed walls, punch and gouge architecture, and beautiful rugs. The staff dressed in red tops and black bottoms, appeared to be very busy. Dollar sat in the customer seating area and waited to be helped.

"Mr. Dollar I can help you now."

Dollar walked over to the customer satisfaction representative's desk, and sat.

"How may I help you sir?"

"I need to transfer $1,000 to my mother's account. She is ill and needs help with a few things around the house."

"No problem sir. Let me complete the paperwork, and I will bring it back for you to review and sign. Since it is early, this wire transfer will go out today. I am sorry to hear about your mother."

The customer service representative stood and walked away to complete the paperwork.

"He hollered at me on purpose!," a voice exclaimed. "Nothing you can say will make me believe otherwise. He is talking to me this way because I am poor. He wants to hurt my feelings. He does not want me in the credit union."

The manager, Mr. Beecher, listened to the upset customer; then, he asked the customer to step into his office. He allowed the customer to calm down before interrupting her and possibly causing more of a scene.

The representative assisting Dollar returned in 20 minutes for Dollar to sign the paperwork.

"Mr. Dollar, I am sorry for the commotion. That customer bounces checks totaling over $300 all of the time and wants the credit union to pay the checks. She does not have over draft protection attached to her checking account. When I say bounces checks all of the time, I mean almost every other week. Furthermore, that weekly check bouncing complaining witch never wants to pay the insufficient funds fees. Every week she creates a scene. We need to close her account! Enough about her please review this paper work. One thousand dollars will be transferred from your account to your mother's account today."

Dollar reviewed his name, his mother's name, the numbers to both bank accounts, and the dollar amount, $1000. Everything was in order, and he proceeded to sign the wire transfer form.

"Mr. Dollar is there anything else I may help you with today?"

"No thank you. This transfer is all I need. Will it get to my mother today?"

"Yes it will, Sir."

Dollar stood and left the credit union. Since the day turned out so nice he went to his car to get his lap-top computer, and decided to walk to the bagel shop to get a bite to eat. The shop has WI-FI, therefore he could review emails, and complete some work while sitting in the bagel shop. After all, he left the house as fast as he could in order to get to the credit union by the time it opened.

"I'll have a cinnamon raisin bagel with strawberry cream cheese and a large coffee with three creams."

Dollar received his food and sat down to eat. Noticing a newspaper on the table he decided to read it to determine the latest happening in Washington, D.C. Immediately he noticed a workshop on the topic of customer service. The workshop would be held the following month. After reading the description, Dollar realized the workshop covered the same general topics he had seen previously. The workshop did not document the teachings from any specific examples, nor detail procedures to move past poor customer service.

While sitting reading the newspaper and sipping his coffee Dollar's cell phone rang.

"Hello," answered Dollar.

"Sir my name is Mr. Smith. I am an instructor at a school in a neighboring state. I sent an email to you about a newly forming high school banking curriculum. I am on the committee to develop the curriculum for this business banking program. The curriculum will include entrepreneurship, marketing, and management courses. It will contain advanced math courses, as well. I am asking your assistance in helping to develop specific banking courses that will catapult this program as a secondary institutional leader in business education, moreover banking."

"Mr. Smith I received your email and proposal; I will be delighted to work with the program. I am an officer at SBNA and have worked in banking over ten years. As you know the bank sponsors a company wide volunteer program.

After reading your correspondence and proposed curriculum, I knew I wanted to play a part in the developmental stages. I noticed one area of the curriculum to further develop. That area is customer service. The program defines and maps the mechanics of each course. I was able to ascertain the students would be taught numerous mechanical and cognitive intricacies surrounding the noted courses.

One subject needing infusion into each subject is customer service. The students' need to know that implemented mechanical and cognitive skills, without the accompaniment of emotional intelligence, is a recipe for disaster.

Currently, the bank is in the process of revamping its training and development program to include more development. We have learned training is more than standing before an audience lecturing. There has to be reading, role playing, and follow-up sessions. Furthermore, there has to be an understanding of pre-seminar and post seminar knowledge.

As a bank in the business of customer oriented growth, we will be happy to help develop the program's curriculum. We have experienced students leaving high school and starting entry level positions without understanding the value of customers to a business. We find these workers chewing and cracking gum while talking to customers. Customers are being spoken to in less than professional tones. Customers concerns are not followed-up within a timely manner. Long term friendly customers become unconcerned customers and change banks.

I'd like to see the curriculum developed to the point every course weaves in the value of customers. The learners should gain an understanding from each of the following:

- Customers are vital to the business
- Speak to customers in a pleasant tone at all times
- Speak clearly
- Chewing gum and eating before customers are negatives
- Customers should not stand at the counter and wait for employees to complete personal conversations
- The work environment should be neat and orderly

- Customers should be listened to without preconceived notions
- Eye contact is important
- When encountering a highly concerned customer get a supervisor to assist
- Do not retaliate with negative words and tones
- Customer service representatives should be able to respond immediately to customer demands
- Customer service representatives must be able to respond to the expectations of all generations

Mr. Smith, I have mentioned some key items the bank deems as necessary to support the program. I will review my calendar tomorrow then send a meeting planner to you so that we may discuss this program in more detail."

"Thank you," said Mr. Smith. "I'll look forward to receiving the meeting planner."

"I am glad my friends and I decided to pay particular attention to the topic of customer service this month," thought Dollar. I am really surprised the representative helping me discussed the other customer's concerns so readily. I wonder if my personal affairs are discussed with other customers. Maybe I need to close my accounts at the credit union."

Looking at the clock on the wall Dollar noticed the time was 2:30 PM. He had read the newspaper thoroughly, reviewed 100 emails, and completed a project for work due by Tuesday. Dollar decided to call his mom to tell her to contact her bank to verify if the money had been deposited into her account.

"Hello mom. I deposited money into your account. I'll call your bank and connect the call as a three-way call. You will need to ask about your deposit for $1,000."

After several rings, Dollar and his mother heard, "Thank you for calling the Credit Union. How may I help you?"

"My name is Fannie Mae Bill. Has a deposit been made to my account for $1,000?"

"Hello Mrs. Dollar. How are you today? This is Sherrie."

"Hello Sherrie. I am fine. And you?"

"Mrs. Bill, I am fine. I know this is you, yet I need to verify your account. What are your mother's maiden name, and your birth date?"

Mrs. Bill verified her account. She lives in a small town in Georgia with a population of approximately 5058 people. Everyone seems to know each other.

"Mrs. Bill I see a deposit, but the deposit is for $10 and not $1,000. Let me look into the situation and call you back."

"Okay. I'll wait for you to call me back, Sherrie."

"Mom, let me call my bank and determine what has happened. I'll call back, also."

Dollar called his credit union and asked to speak to the representative he spoke with earlier in the day.

"Hi, my name is Dollar Bill. I worked with you this morning to get $1,000 wired to my mother's account. I called my mother and learned that only $10 reached her account. Will you check into this matter for me?"

"First of all Sir, you will have to come in and complete some forms. We will be closing in 15 minutes. If you are not on the way here now, you will have to come tomorrow. I cannot keep the doors open until you get here," said the representative. She hung up the telephone and continued. "These customers are a trip. They want you to do everything."

Dollar was devastated. He took off today in order to help his mother. As he sat thinking of his next move, he decided to wire money through the check cashing station. This would cost more, but his mother needed the money.

On the way to the check cashing station, Dollar thought about the behavior of the representative at the credit union. He thought, "Should I call the manager and report her, or should I move my accounts to another financial institution? The representative does not seem to understand customer confidentiality. This credit union should review its customer service training and development program. I am starting to see too many negative situations. I wonder if the Credit Union employs the services of secret shoppers to open accounts, conduct transactions, and etcetera to ensure the quality of the representatives' services."

The buzzing telephone brought Dollar out of his trance. Reaching for the telephone, he said, "Hello."

"Mr. Dollar Bill, it is Sherrie from your mother's bank. I have researched the wire transfer situation. The $1,000 is now in your mother's account. I have her on the phone."

"Thank you so much," said Dollar. "I was about to grab my check book and run into the check cashing station to send more money."

"I called your credit union and spoke to the wire transfer manager. It seems as though the clerk at your credit union input $10 into the system to be transferred instead of $1,000. The manager at your credit union corrected the situation quickly. She told me she would call you to apologize for the error. The good thing is your mother has been taken care of."

"Thank you so much," said Dollar. "Hello mom."

"Hello Dollar," said his mother. "You know this has been my bank for over 20 years. They always look out for me here. Sherrie has been a big help."

"Yes," said Dollar. He began to think, "My mother's bank seems to know, understand, and employ quality customer service representatives. Sherrie seems to have the ability to solve no-nonsense customer concerns and deal with a mixture of concrete variables in situations where a small degree of standardization exists. She exhibits the aptitude to understand a variety of instructions delivered in written, oral, diagram, or schedule form. Her training was demonstrated in her calling my credit union and getting the manger involved so my mother would receive her money on time. Sherri is a leader. She refused to accept the status quo of financial politics."

Dollar thought, "This incident reminds me of when I worked in the Quality Assurance department. Some companies refer to it as the User Acceptance Testing department. One key project was to test the programming of a major credit card that is used internationally. This credit card product was new to our bank and expected to increase revenue by over one million dollars within a year. I was accustomed to documenting projects and ensuring every script tested could be re-tested and receive the same results under the same testing circumstances. This credit card project brought on new standard of measure, ISO 9000."

Dollar sipped his water and continued his thought on quality service. "Achieving ISO 9000 certification has benefits. The ISO 9000 standards provide firms openings to boost worth to their activities and to advance their performance repeatedly, by centering on their key processes. The standards focus major importance on moving quality management systems closer to the processes of businesses and on continual enhancement. Thus, businesses direct users to the accomplishments of business results. This result takes into account the satisfaction of customers and other concerned entities. The management team of businesses should be able to understand the implementation of quality management system standards as a profitable business outlay. There should be, if any, a paradigm shift from the thought of ISO 9000 as only a required certification concern. ISO 9000 is the connection of quality management systems to organizational processes. Until ISO, previous efforts to approach quality management were a problem as previous measures addressed compliance without considering the complex dynamics of people and culture. Following a set of guidelines allows for consistency in processes.

ISO 9000, along with the use of quality products and a well educated staff, allowed my team to deliver a quality product with quality processes. Thus we were able to drive enhanced customer service between the businesses."

Questions

1. What are examples of good customer service in this chapter?

2. What are examples of poor customer service in this chapter?

3. What could management have done to prevent the less than stellar customer service ?

4. At what point did customer service at the bank glide towards the boiling frog phenomenon?

5. How could the banking officials have enhanced customer service?

6. How does the implementation of ISO 9000 help a business and its customer service efforts?

Notes

Quote

"You gain strength, courage and confidence by every experience in which you really stop to look fear in the face...You must do the thing you think you cannot do."

By Eleanor Roosevelt

(Chambliss, et al., (1991), p. 47)

Chapter 2

Stu, Higher Education and Customer Service

Tuesday morning arrived with Stu preparing to go to the local university to enroll for courses. Gazing at himself in the bathroom mirror, Stu ran a hand over his thin hairy face and chin. He definitely needed to shave. He applied his special lathering cream and gently moved the razor over his face and chin, rinsed his face, brushed his curly brown hair, and then went into his room to dress while listening to *How Many Times* and *Atonement* by The W.E.S. Group.

By this time Stu was dressed in a pair of black cargo pants with sewn down flaps, and a crisp white shirt. As he put on his black blazer, The W.E.S. Group's *Journey Within* began to play. Stu walked downstairs, through the great room, and into the kitchen. Not wanting to be late he grabbed a quick bite to eat, and ran to his green Oldsmobile Bravada.

While driving to the University Stu pressed the CD player's button so he could listen to more jazz from The W.E.S. Group. He thought about the numerous offices he would have to visit to enroll and be registered.

Thirty minutes passed, Stu arrived at the University, and parked outside of the admissions office in the visitors' parking area. The campus is beautiful with rounded beds of vibrant colored tulips, yellow, red, and violet, approximately three feet deep. The tulip beds sat in grassy noles throughout the campus. Tall pine trees interspersed all over the campus. The grounds gave a sense of peace.

A lump began to fill Stu's throat. It has been ten years since he last stroll any college's halls. Although he was progressing very well at the Grant, Holland, and Peterson Accounting Firm, he finally decided to return to school for a MBA degree. He was excited about returning to school, and in particular, to a large university. Stu completed his undergraduate degree at a smaller college in his home state of Georgia. After graduation he moved to the metropolitan Washington, D.C. area. Attending a university would be a great challenge, and a way to develop long term relationships with the professors, and etc. You see Stu plans to move from the MBA program right into a Ph.D. program.

Stu found himself standing at the counter of the University's bustling admissions office. The garnet and gold sign hanging outside of the door provided the hours of operation.

Office of Admissions
Monday - Thursday 9:00 AM to 7:30 PM
Friday - 9:00 AM to 5:00 PM
Saturday - 9:00 AM to 12 Noon
Sunday – Closed

Startled by a small voice saying and asking, "Hello, how may I help you?" Stu was initially embedded in his own world of thoughts.

Stu replied, "Fine. I am here to apply for admissions into the University."

While loudly chewing and popping gum, the representative pushed an application across the counter, leaned backwards to reach down, picked up her cell phone, then continued what appeared to be a continued personal conversation. She ceased all eye contact with Stu. Even though amazed, and disappointment with this behavior, Stu proceeded to complete, then proof-read the application.

"Ms. I have completed the application." Stu stood, walked across to the counter, and handed the representative the application.

The representative replied, "Okay sir. Have a seat. I will get back to you."

Stu sat as he was told. The chairs were hard and very uncomfortable. Thirty minutes passed and no one called Stu's name. Dismayed, and surprised by this initial encounter, Stu decided to go to the counter and inquire into his application. He stood at the counter fifteen minutes before being acknowledged.

"Sir may I help you?"

"Yes. My name is Stu Jackson. I completed an application for admission into the University over 30 minutes ago, and no one has called my name."

"Let me look for the application."

The second representative looked through piles and piles of applications to no avail.

"Are you sure you completed an application, Sir? Cause I do not see one. If you completed an application it should be here on the counter. Who did you give it to?"

"Ma'am, the lady previously sitting where you are sitting did not give her name. She took my application, asked me to have a seat, and I complied."

"I am going to have to get you to complete another application, Sir. I don't know what she did with your initial application. Here is a blank application. I will need a $30 application fee."

Excitement turned to frustration for Stu as he sat to complete the second application. He was not upset about the application fee. He was disappointed at the level of customer service provided at the admissions counter. As Stu perused the office, he noticed numerous lights missing from the ceiling. The workers in the background, in customer view, chewed and cracked on gum. One man ate a barbeque chicken sandwich while talking to another co-worker. Another employee walked around with a scarf, not a religious symbol, on his head.

Stu thought, "It is amazing the dress code at this institution is at such a reduced level. That scarf is a simple doo-rag many guys wear to bed. This scarf presentation is not at a professional level. Additionally, it does not present a professional image for the school, the student body, or visitors."

Stu's examination of the office was interrupted by "Sir, are you done yet?"

Stu walked the application back to the counter. This second representative completed the application in 15 minutes.

"Mr. Jackson, I am so sorry you had to wait so long. You are in the system now. All you have to do is register for courses. The business department is in the Mitchell building. Your advisor is Dr. Paul Hiers. He will help you get the courses you will need to complete the MBA program."

"Thank-you," said Stu. "I know the location of the building." His thoughts continued. "The overall operation of this office would be much better if the representatives presented themselves more professionally. It would be interesting to know if this group attends seminars focused on the art of service to customers with role play, videos, and etc.

There appears to be no immediate consequences for negative actions because there were so many of them. When I get home, I will write to the Dean and the Division head about my experiences today."

Stu walked over to the Mitchell building, and located Dr. Hiers. Even though the initial experience was tainted, he remained thrilled about returning to school after ten years to get an advanced degree. Stu found Dr. Hiers sitting in his office.

"Good morning Dr. Hiers. My name is Stu Jackson, and I have enrolled into the University to earn a MBA in the field of Accounting. Currently I am a senior accountant at Grant, Holland, and Peterson Accounting Firm here in town."

"Mr. Jackson, welcome to the University. We have a great MBA program. Ninety percent of the University's instructors have over 20 years of experience in their fields. We have had a number of employees from the Grant, Holland, and Peterson accounting firm graduate from this institution. You should find your experiences here rich and rewarding. Let's prepare a list of courses for you. Do you know the department head of the comprehensive course work series for the Accounting Department?

Stu replied, "Dr. J. Anderson is the professor with over 30 years in the field. He has held numerous dynamic positions in Fortune 500 companies. Additionally, he has spear-headed a well known comprehensive curriculum, which is highly regarded in the industry. I have followed his career for some time."

"Great. I know Dr. Anderson. In addition to being a professor here at the University, he is an active published consultant. By the way, don't forget to take your tuition remission paperwork to the Bursars office. I assume the firm is paying the tuition?"

"Yes. The Grant, Holland, and Peterson accounting firm will pay my tuition. The firm offers a great tuition reimbursement program to its employees. Even though I am a senior accountant with demanding hours, the company will work with me while I complete the degree."

Stu received a registered list of courses, then decided to walk to the Bursar's office to ensure he knew the location for future purposes. Upon arrival he noticed the office hours and made a note of them. The garnet and gold sign above the windows provided the hours of operation

Office of the Bursar's
Monday - Thursday 9:00 AM to 4:00 PM
Friday - 9:00 AM to 12:00 Noon
Saturday - Closed
Sunday – Closed

While in the operations center, Stu decided to find the Registrar's office. This office, located one hall away, was open for business. The office hours, highly visible, were listed on a garnet and gold sign above the multiple stations.

Office of Registration & Records
Monday - Thursday 9:00 AM to 9:00 PM
Friday - 9:00 AM to 5:00 PM
Saturday - 9:00 AM to 12:00 Noon
Sunday – Closed

"I like the multiple avenues to register for courses at this university. Advisors are empowered to register students. Students may go to the registration counter to receive a roster for courses, or register on line," thought Stu.

His next walk would be to Streett's bookstore. The bookstore was across campus; however, Stu regained his momentum and resolved to walk the 20 minutes. It is very apparent the schools Horticulture department works hard around the campus. The flowers growing along side the walkways made the campus look beautiful. The tulips stood bending in the slight breeze as if they were waiting all day for such a time to appear before Stu. He finally reached the bookstore.

Entering Streett's, Stu's enthusiasm for school amplified. He thought, "I did it. I am in the MBA program, and about to advance my career."

Stu walked around the store looking for books. After 20 minutes, he saw a sales representative. "Are you able to help me locate some books?"

Without looking up, the representative said, "I don't know. What are you looking for?"

"I am looking for accounting business books," replied Stu. "Here is my list. Will you help me locate these three books."

"Hmmm-huh," the representative muttered with a pen in his mouth. "Hand me the list."

Hearing the representative's muttering, Stu, standing in the center of the bookstore's supply aisle, handed over the book list. The desire to help wasn't pleasant. Nonetheless it was help and

Stu knew he needed to get on the road, get home, and prepare for his budget meeting with the Telephony team on Wednesday.

"Sir, here are you books. Take them over to the register and someone will ring them up for you. I hope you enjoy your courses."

Stu thought, "This book store experience was interesting. The student helping me obviously hasn't been educated in the art of customer service. She never looked up at me. She spoke with the pen in her mouth. She did help me find the books; however, the experience would have been better if she presented herself with a friendlier disposition. More than likely, I would have purchased add-on items such as notebooks, t-shirts, plus pens and pencils with the schools' logo. Today she lost the opportunity to increase her sales. The bookstore lost the opportunity for me to tell 10 or more people that I received great service and suggest that they purchase supplies there. Overall the store is nice. I will give it a second chance."

While walking out of the store with his purchases, Stu decided to look for the bookstore's hours of operation. Streett's Bookstore's signage was large and clear. The garnet and gold sign on the building provided the hours of operation.

Streett's Bookstore
Monday – Friday Thursday 7:30 AM to 10:00 PM
Saturday - 9:00 AM to 5:00 PM
Sunday - 9:00 AM to 2:00 PM

Questions

1. What are examples of good customer service in this chapter?

2. What are examples of poor customer service in this chapter?

3. What are the boiling frog observable facts regarding the University's operations?

4. How could the University officials have enhanced its overall customer service?

5. What could management have done to prevent the less than stellar customer service ?

Notes

Notes

Quote

"These three things - work, will, success - fill human existence. Will opens the door to success, both brilliant and happy. Work passes these doors, and at the end of the journey success comes in to crown one's efforts."

By Louis Pasteur

(Chambliss, et al., p. 48)

Chapter 3

Meaty, Grocery Shopping and Customer Service

On Wednesday morning Meaty and Shopper paired up and decided to hang together for the day. Their first trip would be to the grocery store. The two would venture to a mall or somewhere else to shop later in the day.

"Shopper did you take the grocery list off of the refrigerator?" asked Meaty. "Does it appear to be complete?"

Meaty replied, "Yes, I have the list. It appears as though everyone has noted items to the list and signed-off for the completion of their listings. I am careful to look for everyone's sign-off. One time I took the list before all of our house-mates had the opportunity to note requests. It is good we designated a day for everyone to review the list so that no one's items will be left off. Which grocery store should we go to today Shopper?"

"Let's try the new grocery store, Green's. It is the one in Virginia containing groceries, as well as a restaurant, and all types of ethnic delicacies. This grocery store has representatives demonstrating ways to prepare different foods. Customers may taste small samples of food while walking around the store. The aisles are wider than most grocery stores; therefore, it is easier to maneuver the shopping carts. The store has a wide variety of products. Also, it always has fresh produce and meats. There is a wide variety of fish, as well."

Meaty knew the location of the new grocery store. He had gone there with Dollar a few weeks ago to have lunch. Breakfast, lunch, and dinner are served daily. The store was about 30 minutes from the house.

As they pulled out of the garage onto Bentree Road and headed towards the main road, Meaty and Shopper thought what a beautiful day. The day was the way one would want a May morning to be, bright, clear, and cheerful. Soon they were crossing the Woodrow Wilson Bridge.

They allowed themselves 45 minutes to get to the grocery store. Since there was little traffic they arrived in 30 minutes. They located a parking space near the front of the store, and walked in heading for the restaurant. Both were ravenous. After eating they secured a shopping cart and both headed for the meat department.

As they entered the department they noticed a lady wearing a yellow clam digger set standing in the area. Next appeared a well manicured lady wearing bell bottomed blue jeans and a short sleeve red sweater. She walked up and pulled a number from the number dispenser. Both ladies spoke cordially to each other.

The woman in the clam digger set said, "I did not realize I had to pull a number." She briskly walked over to the dispenser and snatched a number.

After two to three minutes the counter opened. The gentleman behind the counter called out, "Number 77!"

The lady wearing the blue jeans and red short sleeve sweater walked forward and handed the grocer her number. She stood smiling when a clatter arose behind her.

"Wait just a minute Ms. Bell Bottoms!" snarled the lady in yellow. I was here before you! What number do you have? I have number 78. You should have the number 79."

"I am so sorry, I have number 77. I simply walked up to the dispenser and pulled a number. Is there a problem?"

"Yes there is a problem, Ms. Bell Bottoms. I should have had the 77. You pulled your number before I pulled my number. I was in the area before you. You should have asked if I had a number before prancing over to the dispenser like a deer and pulling a number. Some nerve!"

The lady in the bell bottoms maintained her composure. She did not raise her voice or flinch.

"If you would like to go first, go right ahead. I am not in a hurry. The day is pleasant, my goal is to fully enjoy it."

At this point the grocer interrupted and said, "We assist customers in numerical order. The person with the lowest number is the one to be assisted first."

In his mind he thought, "Should I wait on the woman with the number 78 first?"

After thinking he thought he had better take them in order. Once he assisted a customer with a higher number because the customer with the lower number agreed. Later the store manager called him into the office and showed him a letter of complaint from the woman with the lower number. At that point, he was told to always wait on customers in numerical order.

Meaty and Shopper watched this display until it was over. Both shook their heads as they walked away in disbelief.

"Interesting, wasn't it Meaty? People can be difficult to understand. I thought the lady in the yellow would realize she should have pulled a number as soon as she entered the department. All of the grocery stores in the area have this system in place. What do you think the problem was?"

"Shopper, the lady in the yellow seems to have been having a bad day, and did not know how to control her emotions. She never said I am sorry or anything close to it. I wonder what type of behavior she displays in general. I have seen other people like her who will drag you down and drain the energy out of you with their less than desirable personalities."

"You know, Shopper, customer service is an exchange of behavior. It has elements of verbal and nonverbal communications. The lady in the yellow did not display a positive attitude from the beginning. She never smiled, and her tone remained harsh throughout the entire ordeal. The grocer definitely had himself a difficult situation. Even though the ladies were not exchanging goods, they did exchange non-verbal and verbal communications. The lady wearing the blue jeans actions are great examples of how one may contain his or her composure even in the midst of negative behavior. This situation is surely a matter to discuss at our next team meeting."

Meaty and Shopper completed shopping at the meat counter, picked up a few other items, then preceded to the check-out. While checking out the items, a bag of nut mix rang up its regular price as opposed to the sale price. Meaty informed the clerk of the item being on sale.

"Sir, this item is not on sale. It is regular price. I think it was on sale last week." She placed the nut mixture in a bag.

"Ma'am, there is a sale sign next to this nut mix. I want to get the price noted on the sign," said Meaty.

The clerk continued, "The item is no longer on sale. I can take it off your grocery bill, or leave it in your bag. Which do you want me to do? I can not change prices in the register to accommodate you."

While Meaty was attempting to convince the clerk of the sale price, Shopper walked to the aisle and returned with the sale sign.

"Here is the sign, Ma'am," said Shopper.

"As I said. The item may have been on sale; however, it is no longer on sale. I can read my computer. It shows me the item is no longer on sale. There is nothing I can do about the pricing. You will have to wait until the nut mix is on sale if you want a bag."

By this time the manager noticed the line was not moving, and walked over to the clerk's register. As soon as the manger appeared, Meaty began to explain the dilemma. The manager listened to Meaty's concern, looked at the sale's advertisement, and then adjusted the regular price to the sale price.

"Sir, I am so sorry about the mishap. I have given you the sale price. Again, I am sorry. I, as well as the management staff of this grocery store, value each and every customer. We want your shopping experience to be the best every time you come into the store. I have placed your bags in the shopping cart. If you have any additional questions, let me know. Please come back again."

"I will return to Green's grocery store," said Meaty.

Meaty and Shopper walked out to their vehicle. Meaty pressed the button on the key fob to open the trunk. Shopper placed the meats and milk in the coolers, and the other groceries on the floor of the trunk. He closed the trunk, got into the car with Meaty, and they started the drive home. Meaty pressed the power button on the CD player, and pushed the select button until he reached the tune *Ballard for Ethan* by The Will Smith Quartet and Co.

"Shopper, we experienced a mixture of experiences in the grocery store. The actions of the clerk reminded me of the ole' false tale about domesticated turkeys. The story goes at the first drop of rain, a turkey will look up into the rain with its mouth open. It will stand with it mouth open until it drowns. The likeness is the clerk never bothered to seek another direction in her thoughts about the mixed nuts. She continued to affix her thoughts on the idea the mixed nuts were not on sale. I believe her behavior is a result of social apathy. She exhibits no understanding or perception of other people's feelings, nor does she display the ability to work with and bring forth the wanted response in customers.

Stretching his arms out while pressing his palms forward, Shopper yawned and said, "You are correct. People run through their days in routine. They do not appear to think or care. Every now and then a person may hear something to make someone smile, and think, I wish I had been the person to bring the smile. Within minutes of the caring thought, there is the group of individuals who are back to moving without thinking.

Whether the behavior is a lack of caring or a lack of thinking, the end result to the customer is the same."

"Shopper have you decided where you want to go shopping?"

"Yes. I need to return some jeans to the Ten East store at the mall by the house."

The rest of the ride was spent listening to tunes by The W.E.S. Group. The two reached their home on Bentree Road, and rushed to put the groceries away. Soon they were back in the car heading to the mall and listening to The Will Smith Quartet and Co.'s tune *When Orinthology Met Sugarhill.*

Questions

1. What are examples of good customer service in this chapter?

2. What are examples of poor customer service in this chapter?

3. At what point did customer service at the grocery store lean towards the boiling frog phenomenon?

4. How could the grocery store management have enhanced customer service?

5. What could management have done to prevent the less than stellar customer service ?

Notes

Notes

Quote

"To be successful, the first thing to do is fall in love with your work."

Sister Mary Lauretta

(Chambliss, et al., p. 57)

Chapter 4

Shopper, Retail Shopping and Customer Service

Shopper and Meaty arrived at the mall. They decided to park on the opposite end of where the store is located in order to get some extra exercise for the day. While walking past the music store they both paused as they heard the tune, *All the Fire,* by The W.E.S. Group.

After the tune stopped playing, they walked down the mall into the store, Ten East. Shopper and Meaty both looked for the pants Shopper really wanted. The store was clean, orderly, and well stocked. Within 20 minutes each found a pair, and they walked towards the return counter for Shopper to make the exchange.

"May I help you," said a voice from behind the counter.

"Yes. I purchased two pair of jeans. They do not fit and I want to exchange them for another size. The smaller pants are in this bag."

With a solemn face the sales clerk listened without looking up. She grabbed the bag at both bottom ends and shook it until the pants fell onto the counter. After checking the pants to determine whether the tags were still affixed to them, she started to process the exchange through the register. After five minutes of pressing keys, and frowning she said, "You owe $12."

"Twelve dollars!" exclaimed Shopper. "Why?"

The clerk asked Shopper, "You did not think the pants would be free did you?" as she continued to snarl.

In a soft voice Shopper said, "No, I did not think the pants would be free. I did expect an even exchange. Is the manager here?" asked Shopper.

The clerk muttered, "Yes she is. She is going to tell you the same thing I told you. You need to pay $12. Jennie, come over here to help this guy. He is getting on my last nerve!"

The manager approached the area. She looked Shopper and Meaty up and down, then asked the sales clerk, "What is the problem?"

This guy dropped this bag on the counter and asked to exchange these pants. While chewing gum she said, I rang the exchange and the register shows a balance of $12. He does not want to pay," said the clerk.

"Sir, the sale is $12. Do you want to pay by cash, check, or charge?" asked the manager.

Ma'am my name is Shopper. I am here to exchange two pairs of pants for a larger size. The pants are the same brand and style. Why do I have to pay an additional $12?"

The manager stood and pondered. She looked at both sets of pants. She reviewed Shopper's initial register receipt. After a few strokes of the register, she pushed the unfolded pants into a shopping bag. The legs of the pants peeped from the top of the bag. She then handed Shopper the bag and said, "Here are your pants." Without saying anything else, she left the counter and walked into the stock room.

Shopper and Meaty looked at each other in amazement. As they left the store, a floor representative said, "Thank you all for coming. I am sorry about the mishap. Please come again."

"What has happened to customer service?" said Shopper. "There were no smiles. Initially no one said thank you. No one introduced themselves. The manager, the leader, of all people, handed me the bag with the pants hanging out of the top of the bag. It is obvious this bag is too small for these two pairs of pants. The manager displayed no actions to indicate that I was wanted as a customer. I spent $100 for these jeans. There is no real leadership in the store. This business is in need of professional development on the art of service to customers."

Meaty replied, "You are so right. There was no empathy, no passion to serve, no desire to achieve, and no apparent love for the business. Love for the business will help to drive the desire to be the best in the business. The manager's display of customer service was no better than the clerk's. As a leader the manager should have been able to guide the clerk through the right steps and behavior by demonstrating the appropriate customer service words, and behaviors."

Meaty continued, "The world is becoming more dependent upon open communications and the understanding of communications. Emphasis is being placed on leadership, and political correctness. From the CEO to line employees, there must be the understanding of the significance of leadership. A leader is "someone who has commanding authority or influence." Another definition of leader is "any person who influences individuals and groups within an organization, helps them in the establishment of goals, and guides them toward achievement of those goals, thereby allowing them to be effective (Nahavandi, 2003, p. 4)." Leadership is at all levels.

Political changes affect what the world sees and understands as correct leadership. This leadership changes over time. What may have been appropriate twenty years ago is no longer appropriate. The workplace is now more diverse. Organizations are working with more diverse customers. Leadership must make sure these diverse customers are able to be served by an understanding team of employees. In assisting team members to achieve desired results, management may seek organization politics. "Organization politics are activities by which people seek to improve their positions within the organization, generally by gaining power" (Certo, p. 412). At this point let me say improving the position is not the key here. Political skill is the key. This skill will "help a supervisor," or any member of management "obtain the cooperation and support of others in the organization" (Certo, p.412). This corporation can drill down to the leaders' team members. According to Nahavandi, "leaders are caretakers of their teams, helping them achieve their goals by providing them with instructions, encouragement when needed, and resources" (p.208).

Shopper replied, "The manager did not show herself as a good care take of her team. The clerk at the register needs a seminar or course on anger control. In previous courses I learned to take a mental pause and deep breath before speaking when engaged in a potentially negative conversation. I had a legitimate concern that was handled poorly. Situations are not always smooth, and representatives should know how to handle multiple types of customer concerns. Customer retention and loyalty is important to repeat business, and to remain competitive. This incident at Ten East will be a scenario to discuss when we all reconvene to discuss our individual customer service experiences."

Questions

1. What are examples of good customer service in this chapter?

2. What are examples of poor customer service in this chapter?

3. At what point did customer service at Ten East slant towards the boiling frog phenomenon?

4. How could the Ten East management have enhanced customer service?

5. What could management have done to prevent the less than stellar customer service ?

6. What is the potential for business profits and customer retention if more customers are treated as Shopper was treated?

7. Review the behavior of Ten East's manager and staff. How can this store establish itself as a top quality customer service retailer within the mall?

Notes

Notes

Quote

"Every person must have a concern for self, and feel a responsibility to discover one's mission in life...Potential powers of creativity are within us, and we have a duty to work assiduously to discover these powers."

Martin Luther King, Jr.

(Chambliss, et al., p. 16)

Chapter 5

Peachie, Dining and Customer Service

Peachie awaken on Thursday with a start. She sat straight up, reached out her hand to turn on the lamp, and looked at the alarm clock. The time was nine in the morning. Today is to be a busy one for she has plenty of work to complete to prepare for a work meeting tonight. Peachie is an engineering consultant and has a regional meeting tonight about an hour from the house. In addition to the meeting, today is her day to take a hard look at customer service. While at the meeting she would attempt to complete her customer service project.

Peachie gathered her thoughts, showered, dressed, and headed to the kitchen to get something to eat. Peachie first went to the great room to turn on the stereo. She loved to listen to jazz music, and selected the CD, The W.E.S. Group, and in particular the track, *The Spirit of You*. She then headed to the kitchen. Decorating the kitchen had been her project when the team moved into the house.

The walls were cream with an earth colored floor tile. The light pine wood cabinets glistened against golden knob handles. The counter tops accented the floor with speckles of multi-colored earth tones. The back splash just above the counter tops were of the earth toned family, as well. The hint of gold sheers decorating the windows blended well and allowed the sunlight to shine through all year.

Peachie noticed the wonderful smells of cheese grits, fresh baked raisin biscuits, cinnamon apples, and coffee wafting through the air. With each sniff she grew hungrier and hungrier. Peachie prepared a plate with everything and sat down to eat.

"I love this breakfast," she thought.

Peachie sipped her coffee, took a piece of warm biscuit, spread it with soft butter and homemade blackberry jelly, and then took a bite. Her mind drifted to the work she needed to complete for the dinner meeting later in the evening and to the customer service project.

She could hear BATS giving his customer service message on Sunday night. "Customer service is the ability or skill to service a customer with a smile. Moreover, customer service is timely delivery, great service, strong support, a representative able to work with all types of customers, and the catalyst extending to repeat business and referrals."

After eating Peachie walked upstairs to her office in the loft. The space had become her sanctuary. No one else wanted the space due to the angled roof. Peachie decorated it and loved the open space. She furnished the loft sparingly. The biggest expense for the loft was the stereo speakers she had wired into the walls so she could listen to jazz as she worked.

"This customer service project is a good one," she thought. "So many times I have gone to businesses and have been treated as thought the business was doing me a favor to be there. Tonight it will be interesting to observe and note the outcome. Let me write some key points to observe."

Peachie noted several points to observe:

- Quality of service
- Quality of the food
- Friendliness of the server(s)
- Friendliness of the hostess
- Knowledge of the sommelier

- Accurateness of the reservation

Peachie reviewed her list then focused on her work for the day.

The phone rang. Startled Peachie looked towards the clock. The time was 3:30 PM. She needed to arrive at Chez Johnson's no later than 6:45 PM. She saved her documents, turned off the computer, then ran down the steps to get dressed. By 5:00 PM, Peachie was in her car driving to the meeting. She needed to leave early in order to fill her vehicle with gas and ensure she arrived for dinner with her co-workers by 6:45 PM.

Peachie arrived at the restaurant just in time. Her co-workers were all dressed in dark colored suits, white shirts, and magnificent accenting ties. Robed in a couture black tea length dress, and jacket with a set of freshwater pearl earrings, and matching necklace, all eyes were on Peachie. She picked up her briefcase as the porter opened her car door. Next she handed him the keys, placed the parking ticket in her purse, and then walked to the restaurant's door.

"I need to start my observations now," Peachie thought.

She walked into Chez Johnson's restaurant and the hostess said, "Good evening ma'am. My name is Ledora. May I have the name of the party you are with?"

"Good evening. I am with the Cartwright Consulting Group," said Peachie.

"Please follow John, he will direct you to your party. Have a nice dinner."

"Please allow me to show you to your seat," stated John.

"So far, so good," thought Peachie as she followed John.

The restaurant was large with recessed lighting and plenty of greenery. A black shiny baby grand piano stood proudly encircled in more greenery. Each thick dark wood claw footed table covered with a white linen cloth bore the look of elegance. The hostesses wore all black. The waiters and waitresses wore white tops and black bottoms. The smell of tasty food permeated the air.

"Your party is in here, the Delaware room, ma'am."

Peachie walked into the room. The team, circulating and chatting before dinner, appeared lively. Peachie joined in.

"Good evening team," sounded a voice from the front of the Potomac room.

It was her project leader. He opened the dinner and everyone sat. The waiters and waitresses all lined up at the door in perfect formation, one per employee, were prepared to serve. The master sommelier entered the room and gave a message about the wine for the day. He poured five ounces into the project leader's crystal goblet, waited for the leader to swirl the wine in his goblet, sniff it, and then give the okay to serve the team. The leader approved. Next the sommelier gave the nod for the waiters, and waitresses to serve. They gracefully encircled the tables to perform their crafts. Each time a server left the table and returned, the server reappeared to almost the same position, akin to the Antarctic Adelie penguin, which returns to the same colony of rocks every year, and many times the same position. This level of service represents well thought through planning by the management team.

After about fifteen minutes, the food was served. The waiters and waitresses immediately removed empty dishes. They were prepared to keep the goblets filled throughout the night. Crumbs were consistently removed from the table. All evening, the waiters' and waitresses' service movements were reminiscent of a synchronized dance team.

After the dinner Peachie proceeded to drive home. Twenty minutes into the drive her cell phone rang. She pressed the speaker button then answered.

"Hello."

"Hello Peachie, this is BATS. We all decided to go out for dinner. We know you had dinner with you co-workers; still, we though you may want to join us for conversation."

"Where are you all located BATS?"

"Come to The Warf on the river. We are at our usual table."

"I am almost there," thought Peachie. "I am happy they did not call me any later."

She arrived to The Warf and found her roommates at their usual table.

"How long have you all been here?" asked Peachie.

"We arrived about one and a half hours ago," said Dollar. "The food is great as usual."

In the middle of the conversation a waitress walked by and placed something on the table. The roommates kept talking.

"How have the customer service adventures been?" asked BATS. "Please don't give all of the details until Saturday."

"I went out on Monday and have a host of experiences to share," said Dollar.

"I went out on Tuesday," said Stu. "The day was filled with mixed emotions to say the least."

"Meaty and I went out on Wednesday," said Shopper. We enjoyed the day and have plenty of information to share."

"As you all know today is my day," said Peachie. "So far so good. I am still taking mental notes."

"Tomorrow is my day," said Medic. I have several appointments and plan to take plenty of notes. It has been 20 minutes. Where is our waitress?"

"What is this on the table?" asked Stu.

"It looks like the bill Stu!" exclaimed Meaty. "When was this placed here?"

"I can't believe the waitress left the bill on the table. She never asked if we wanted anything else!" shrieked Peachie. "I am thirsty. Let's locate our waitress."

While looking around no one saw the waitress.

"Oh look," said BATS. "There is a waiter. Let's get his attention." BATS waived for the waiter.

"Yes sir." The waiter asked, "May I help you?"

"Yes, we were looking for our waitress."

" I am so sorry. She left for the evening. I am here to serve you. It was my understanding she let you all know. Don't worry I am here to serve you."

The roommates were happy and upset at the same time.

"I can't believe she did not say anything. We have been coming to this restaurant over two years and have not experienced anything like this," said Stu.

"We appreciate your help, sir; still, we would like to see the manager," said Peachie in a low voice. " I can't believe the service has deteriorated to this level."

The manager arrived to the table previously versed on the situation by the waiter.

"Hello. My name is Russ. I am the night manager. I understand your waitress went home without saying anything. However, we have a waiter here to serve you."

The manager left the room without saying anything else.

"Well," said Peachie. "I don't think I like the way he handled this situation. He never apologized for her leaving and not telling us. How rude is it to leave a bill on the table for a party whom has not finished? We spend over $200 here per week."

"Let's pay this bill and leave," said Dollar. "Let's find another restaurant to frequent. We do not have to spend our money here and be treated like second class citizens. It is obvious the management team does not understand their examples of customer service influences their employees' behavior."

"Let's talk about influence," said BATS. "What is influence? Influence is 'power exerted over the minds or behavior of others' (Webster's Ninth New Collegiate Dictionary, 1989, p. 620). 'When employees trust their leader, they are more willing to engage in voluntary behaviors that benefit the organization' (Podskoff et al, 2000, p513). In the case of this restaurant, the voluntary behavior is providing great customer service."

BATS continued, "This restaurant is clean, the hostesses are nice; however, the management has changed. As time goes on the staff will more than likely mirror the management."

"I agree with all you," said Dollar.

"Let's go," said Peachie.

The team paid the bill and left the restaurant.

Questions

1. What are examples of good customer service in this chapter?

2. What are examples of poor customer service in this chapter?

3. At what point did customer service at either restaurant tilt towards the boiling frog phenomenon?

4. How could the management of the second restaurant have enhanced customer service?

5. What could management have done to prevent the less than stellar customer service?

6. Even though restaurant management and owners must keep their eyes on the bottom-line, at what point could such endeavors effect customer service ?

Notes

Notes

Quote

"Ideas won't keep. Something must be done about them."

Alfred North Whitehead

(Chambliss, et al., p. 18)

Chapter 6

Medic, the Medical Industry and Customer Service

Friday arrived and Medic knew today was his day to observe and note customer service. He was experiencing a spring cold, and was going to the doctor today. He prepared to get to the doctor's office by 8:00 AM.

It was a beautiful May day, very iridescent. The foliage displayed a gradual change from gold and red to shades of green. Medic indulged in the sights of the scenery in their yard on Bentree Road, thinking how glorious everything appeared today. Such stunning colors were all around. The sky was an awe-inspiring blue, without any clouds.

Medic took a moment to sit on the porch in the oversized rocker and appreciate the scenery. He rested his head against the rocker, closed his eyes, and enjoyed the kindness of the sun on his face. Even though achy, he felt calm, and tranquil. Medic gathered his thoughts, arose from the rocker, got into his vehicle, and drove away.

Medic got into his vehicle, inserted a CD by The W.E.S. Group, drove up Bentree Road, made his way to Branch Avenue, and turned onto Pennsylvania Avenue to the doctor's office. Medic's primary care physician relocated to Delaware a few months ago. Medic decided to try this new doctor out for the first time.

A bit nervous, he pressed the door's handle, pushed it open, and walked into the office. Whilst stepping into the office from the foyer Medic noticed the office emerged gray, dim, and generally lackluster. The walls were barely dressed with pictures, or certificates. The appearance of the office suffered from the lack of character. Fine layers of dust rested on the pictures, cabinets, and television. Medic maneuvered through the rows of toys lying topsy turvy amid the floor while walking towards the receptionist's desk.

"This is not what I expected," thought Medic.

He approached the receptionist window to find her sitting behind the sliding glass window eating her breakfast. Startled by Medic, she quickly placed her sandwich on her plate.

With food in her mouth the receptionist stated, "Good morning. May I help you sir?"

Medic placed his name on the patients' sign-in sheet, then stood a few seconds to get his bearings.

"Yes, my name is Medic Coates. I am here to see the doctor. I am a new patient, and previously one of Dr. Pat's patients. She relocated to another state," said Medic.

"Sir, please complete the papers on this clip board. Read and sign the HIPPA statement. Return the papers to me when you are done," said the receptionist. "I will need your insurance card, also."

"This office is not what I am accustomed," thought Medic.

Medic sat down to complete the paperwork. About the time he had almost completed the paperwork, he noticed a man walking slowly into the door. The man made his way to the counter, and began to speak in a low raspy voice.

"I am sick and I need to see the doctor. I do not have any insurance."

"Sir, please complete the papers on this clip board. Read and sign the HIPPA statement. Return the papers to me when you are done. Oh! This visit will be $175," said the receptionist.

Leaning forward while holding onto the counter, the man said, "I do not have $175."

"Sir, today's visit will be $175 unless you have insurance."

"Ma'am, I do not have $175. I am sick. I need to see the doctor."

"Sir, since you do not have $175 or an insurance card, you will need to go to Evan's hospital. Evan's hospital is equipped to assist patients without insurance," said the receptionist.

The sick man's voice lowered, "Ma'am, I have no money. I have no way to get to Evan's hospital. I am very sick. My chest is tight. I feel achy and dizzy. I really need to see the doctor."

"Sir, please complete the paperwork, and have a seat," said the receptionist.

Looking at his watch, Medic realized 20 minutes had passed.

He thought, "I am happy the receptionist asked the sick man to have a seat. I was thinking she was going to turn him away. She did listen to him, and I am elated. I guess the office's rule is to attempt to turn patients without insurance away, and if the patient is persistent, the office will service them."

Medic completed his paperwork and returned it to the counter. A different voice behind the desk said, "May I have your name, and your insurance card sir?"

"Yes," replied Medic, while reaching into his pocket to retrieve the insurance card from his wallet.

"Oh here is my information," said Medic. "Oh my," thought Medic. There is something sticky in my pocket and it is all over my wallet. As soon as I finish at this desk I'll go into the restroom to get something to clean my wallet."

"Ms. Jones, please come this way to see the doctor," echoed a voice from the doorway.

Medic thought, "The carpet in this office smells sour. Food stains are all over the counter behind the receptionist's window."

He walked to the restroom to get a damp paper towel.

As soon as Medic opened the door to the restroom he thought, "This restroom reeks of strong cleanser combined with a stench. There is no soap to clean my hands or wallet, and no

85

paper towels either. Additionally there is no automatic hand dryer. I will be sure to tell my house-mates about this office. I am sure they will not want to have this office as a primary care physician. Even though the office does not have the appearance of cleanliness, the staff seems friendly. On the other hand, I need more than a friendly staff to continue coming here. I am not feeling well, at all. I will be seen by the doctor today; however, I will find another doctor. This office is definitely not for me."

"Medic, come this way please. The doctor will see you now."

Medic walked through the entrance where the nurse directed him. He walked into the examination room and sat while the nurse took his blood pressure and temperature. Medic was quickly seen by the doctor; then he returned to the reception desk to get his prescriptions and follow-up instructions provided by the physician. The receptionist quietly provided the necessary information. Medic proceeded to leave the office. While walking through the waiting area, Medic noticed the sick man still sitting in the waiting room.

"I hope the doctor is able to see that man soon. He doesn't look well at all," thought Medic. "Thank goodness the receptionist did not repeat my follow-up instructions loud enough for everyone in the waiting area to hear."

In the midst of his thoughts, the drug representative walked in. She was loaded down with numerous brief cases. As did Medic, the representative had to maneuver her way through the maze of toys lying all over the floor, as well.

"Hello Sir, my name is Kia. And your name?"

"My name is Medic. Watch your step. Have a great day."

Medic contemplated, "You would have thought someone would have picked the toys up from the floor by now. One of the patients is likely to fall. This office is interesting. The staff is nice and friendly; on the other hand, the appearance of the office leads me to believe the patient care may be lacking."

He left the office with several prescriptions and walked to his vehicle. The parking lot was full of leaves, and vehicles needing repair.

Medic thought, "I overheard one of the staff members answering the phone. As soon as she asked, "May I help you hold? Can you hold?," she was taking another call. Such telephone practices are very irritating. I like to say whether I can hold or not. This office needs phone etiquette education."
Medic got into the vehicle and drove to the pharmacy. He reached the pharmacist. The sign on the building read, Apothecary's.

Medic took his prescriptions to the counter of the Apothecary's, and was immediately greeted.

"Good morning Sir. How may I help you?"

"Good morning. I have several prescriptions to be filled. Here is my prescription card. I may be on file. I generally go to your branch in Virginia by my job," said Medic.

"Thank you Sir. I will look for the record. Please have a seat. Your prescriptions should be ready in 15 minutes."

Questions

1. What are examples of good customer service in this chapter?

2. What are examples of poor customer service in this chapter?

3. At what point did customer service at the medical facility tilt towards the boiling frog phenomenon?

4. How could the restaurant management have enhanced customer service?

5. What could the doctor have done to prevent the less than stellar customer service ?

6. How might the appearance of the parking lot hinder the doctor's business?

7. What opportunities does this doctor's office have to increase its customer flow?

Notes

Notes

Quotes

"Success is not the measure of a man but a triumph over those who choose to hold him back."

Bill Clinton

(Bill Clinton Quotes., (n.d.). Think Exist.com)

Chapter 7

BATS, Orchestrating the Team's Meeting

BATS looked up from the document he was reading and noticed the time, 3:30 PM. The roommates previously planned to meet at 4:00 PM in the great room to discuss the week's adventure of seeking quality customer service. BATS decided to prepare a tray of snacks for the team.

The team gathered at 4:00 PM; the meeting began with BATS as the meeting leader.

"Hello everyone. I am sure this has been an interesting week for us all. Let me reiterate the assignment. Each of us was to go out and seek quality customer service. At the end of the week we decided to discuss each of our findings. Our findings should enable us to prepare several workshops about customer service. The overall goal is to seek avenues to rekindle the art of service to customers across business types and institutions," said BATS.

Excited about the project, the team listened intently.

BATS continued, "Dollar, please tell us about your day."

"I went to the bank and through my encounters documented a host of great and poor customer service experiences. My mother was to be wired $1,000; however, she initially received wired funds of $10. The customer service representative at my credit union did not readily volunteer to investigate the mistake. I am a long term customer of the credit union, and was very disappointed."

"Thank you Dollar," stated BATS. "That customer service representative has a great deal to learn about quality service to customers. I have noted Dollar's experiences in bullet form, as well as the rest of the team's experiences."

Table 1: Dollar

Great Service	Poor Service
• Greeted appropriately by the representative • Wired funds transaction handled timely • Mis-wired funds were researched by Dollar's mother's bank	• The representative discussed upset customer's personal business with Dollar • Wired funds were not received as guaranteed • Wired funds were not initially researched by Dollars bank

"Dollar's credit union has gone through several mergers and acquisitions," said BATS.

"Dollar have you seen the service change over this period of time?" asked Stu.

"Yes. I have seen a gradual decline in overall service. The bank has attempted to mask its deteriorating service by changing its motto from, 'Banking with Excellence,' to 'Banking for the Customer'. The Board of Directors, and officers must take stock of the service they provide to customers. Knowing there is a need for quality customer service, and well educated employees is not enough. Without skilled and well educated employees devoted to quality customer service, all of an organization's efforts to satisfy customers will be futile. There must be a well thought out time and action plan, plus tacticians capable of implementation. Excuses should be avoided at all cost. For "excuses are the tools of incompetence, that build bridges that lead to nowhere. Therefore, to be competent, one must be confident, eliminating excuses to cross bridges that lead to success"(Williams, A.L., (2006). "Message from the Director," Malcolm X College). "Thank you Dollar." BATS continued. "On Tuesday, Stu ventured out to the college and through his day's encounters documented a host of great and poor customer service experiences. Stu please provide us with a synopsis of your day."

Stu began. "I went to the University and experienced numerous levels of customer service. One key focus is the University's operations centers' hours are not consistent to each other. Since these are three intertwined areas, the hours should be similar so all students, those attending during the day, and those attending on evenings and week-ends, may be serviced.

Each manager, as a leader, has to seriously care about the business and its customer base, the student. This commitment to caring needs to consistently trickle down to the staff. Each employee and volunteer in the organization should understand the customer service philosophy and be cognizant of how each of their positions impact quality service. Training and actual practice have to unite again and again and again.

Universities and colleges are institutions of higher learning where people go to advance and/or turn their lives around. Some students immediately go to four year institutions. Others may begin their educational trek at a community college. No matter the size, institutions must provide quality customer service.

Students from all walks of life have to be provided quality service. The students may be external customers, internal customers, or employees of the institution. If quality service can not be appropriately provided to service all students, there will be a serious disconnect in the institutions' abilities to advance and/or turn students' lives around. What has to be maintained is a positive inter-lacing of quality service, enrolled students, and dedicated institutions.

Table 2: Stu

Great Service	Poor Service
• Application was completed by the second representative on a timely basis	• Received first college application from an unprofessional admissions representative
• Empathy was shown by the second representative	• Stu sat for 30 minutes while an application was lost
• Service was provided by the advisor in a timely manner	• Stu was inappropriately greeted at the bookstore
• School offered beautiful surroundings	• The University's operations centers' hours are inconsistent to each other

"Thank you Stu. Quality customer service must remain first."

BATS continued, "Wednesday was Meaty's day to journey out to the grocery store. Even though Shopper went with him, Meaty prepared the notes for the day and emailed them to me. Meaty's day was interesting to say the least. Meaty observed a situation where one customer was accusatory of another. One lady stood still inside of herself and allowed the truth to prevail. The situation he observed was one many people can learn and grow from. The overall message is one negative does not have to be addressed with another negative. Meaty please provide us with a rundown of your day."

Meaty began. "Even though society has changed on many accords, quality customer service remains quality customer service. The customer should leave a business feeling he/she was served efficiently and effectively.

The grocery business has to be able to win in the area of quality service by establishing sound rules of leadership, which lead to service, also. There has to be a strong implementation strategy which includes education and employee buy-in. The business needs to establish metrics to gauge quality customer service. These metric should be at the forefront of the front-line staff, as well as staff members, who are levels from the front-line."

Table three details the great and poor customer service Meaty observed.

Table 3: Meaty

Great Service	Poor Service
• Grocery manager handled the disputing customers with empathy • Store manager immediately price adjusted the mixed nuts • Store manager showed empathy and customer service	• Cashier did not immediately seek help to resolve the sales price concern • Cashier presented a negative attitude to Meaty • Cashier appeared untrained and not empathetic

"Thank you Meaty for your summary."

"Shopper ventured out on Thursday, with Meaty as his partner. He set out to return two pairs of pants to a store in the mall," said BATS. Shopper has some great information to share with the team.

Shopper began. "Thursday was an interesting day. Meaty and I entered the Ten East store and looked around 20 minutes without anyone asking if I needed any help. After finding the pants I needed, the customer service representative did not display the general qualities for the position such as:

- The ability to read and understand documents such as work instruction, procedure manuals, and software manuals
- The ability to add, subtract, multiply, and divide
- The ability to handle problem solving of multiple variables in regards to general sales and/or exchanges
- The ability to present strong customer orientation

Table 4: Shopper

Great Service	Poor Service
• The store was clean, orderly, and well stocked	• No store representative greeted Shopper and Meaty when they entered the store
• The last sale representative thanked Shopper and Meaty for the sale	• The CSR at the register presented a negative attitude and was unable to operate the cash register
• The last sales representative saved Shopper as a customer for the store	• The manager presented a negative attitude and overall presentation

The employees should be provided with "a vision that looks beyond their immediate surroundings" (Nahavandi, 2003, p. 15). Employees look to the next levels of leadership for direction; therefore, leaders will have to remain vigilant of their behavior and statements to change. The result of effective leadership can be quality customer service to each customer; this increases business, and profits.

BATS job is to ensure that every team member has a chance to speak.

"Day four, Thursday, was Peachie's day. She worked from home and was scheduled for a dinner meeting with her co-workers. She later joined us for dinner. Peachie observed several interesting customer service tidbits. Please tell us about them."

Peachie began. "My assignment was to observe customer service in the restaurant business. To say the least, the service at Chez Johnson's was outstanding. The ambiance was serene, the furniture was elegant, the reserved room was spacious, the master sommelier was very knowledgeable, and the food was superb. I was very impressed with the color coordination of the room décor. Hues of blue permeated the dining utensils, the exquisite stemware, the chargers, the china, and even the menus.

The second restaurant, The Warf, was a disappointment. I am not comparing the styles of restaurants for the two are not on the same levels. As customers we were not treated professionally.

The new manager did not exhibit the extraordinary mix of skills and modus operandi successful customer service operations portray. Even though we liked the food, we have decided as a team not to dine there anymore. Quality customer service is very important."

Table 5: Peachie

Great Service	Poor Service
• Employees at Chez Johnson's were very professional in every aspect • Chez Johnson's food, and presentation was superb • The Warf's food was prepared with quality	• The waitress at The Warf lacked communication skills • The manager at The Warf provided poor examples of customer service leadership • Long term customers were made to feel devalued

"Thank you Peachie," said BATS. "Friday, was Medic's day. Since he had to see a physician, his customer service experiences dealt with the medical arena. Medic, please tell us about your day."

Medic began. "I went to a new physician's office because my previous physician relocated her practice to Delaware. I observed the office staff to be nice, but unprofessional. As I approached the receptionist's desk I noticed her eating where customers could see her. She would have served the office better to eat somewhere else. It is great to be nice; however, the office lacked numerous customer service qualities."

Medic continued, "The toys lying all over the floor were miniature disasters waiting to happen. People enter a doctor's office in a less than stellar condition. Someone could have stepped on a toy and seriously injured themselves. Neither the receptionist nor other staff members walked out to remove the scattered toys. The staff was friendly, but unprofessional."

The team gasped at this recounting of Medic's adventure. It appeared as though the management of the doctor's office did not recognize the financial value between a satisfied customer and an unsatisfied customer.

"Medic, have you considered writing the doctor and telling the doctor about your experiences at the office?" asked Peachie. "I am sure the doctor would want to know what is happening and not want customers to leave."

Medic continued. "I will consider writing a letter next week. You are correct Peachie. In order to employ a distinguishing level of quality customer service, the office manager is going to have to realize customers' pre-visit expectations. Service has to positively influence customers' assessments of post-service quality. For example the customer's charts should be pulled prior to their office arrival. Once the customer arrives, insurance information should be confirmed in a tone where only the patient and office staff person hears. Furthermore, the office manager has to make certain the customer's progression of being served is as unproblematic as possible. Customers should feel satisfied after being served.

Table 6: Medic

Great Service	Poor Service
• The receptionist displayed empathy, and was understanding to the sick and indigent man • Medic was serviced in a timely and efficient manner • The staff was very friendly and courteous • Receptionist reiterated the doctor's procedures professionally	• The receptionist was eating at her desk in clear view of customers • The restroom was insufficiently stocked; there was no soap, hand blower, or paper towels • Doctor's office was untidy, and reeked of a foul odor. • Toys lay all over the floor and posed a hazard

"Thank you Medic, said BATS. I'd like to share a customer service experience, also. I am reminded of a transportation incident that occurred on my way to a business trip. I had to catch a plane and decided to park my vehicle at an overnight parking area then board a train to the airport.

I arrived at the overnight parking area, parked my vehicle and, as soon as I was about to step out of the vehicle, rain poured in sheets. Hurriedly I grabbed my belongings out of the trunk and ran to the shelter.

I was surprised and delighted because the shelter was large enough to hold at least 12 people. The shelters I have previously seen are much smaller. The bus arrived on time; the driver was very helpful with placing luggage on the bus. I rode it to the train station with no concerns.

The train ride was quite interesting. A voice unit called out the different stops for the airport. The voice called my stop; I got off the train and proceeded to my gate. Within twenty minutes I learned the train's voice unit was malfunctioning and calling incorrect stops. I encountered at least 15 other people, after getting off the train, and learned they were in the wrong place, also. I, along with the others, returned to the train to get to our intended stops. Thirty minutes later than expected, I arrived at the correct terminal.

Afraid I was about to miss my plane. I ran for the terminal to find a long line. Two friendly and helpful representatives were walking around trying to help over 200 people. The air was filled with voices of confusion and frustration from the many passengers. To my surprise, only two of the airline representatives who were taking luggage displayed smiles and understanding voice tones. I stood in the line over 30 minutes watching the airport representatives and taking notes. My thoughts were, it appears as though this airline has forgotten customers are the driving forces of their business. In order to maintain a larger customer base this airline will have to focus on providing quality customer service.

The train's voice system has been repaired. What hasn't been repaired is the airline's service. I stopped employing the services of that airline as my airline of choice. Several times I have stopped to observe their services and they are no better. I look at this airline and see boiled frog syndrome. This airline appears to be comfortable with its profits; however, its customer base is suffering. As with past empires that were unfocused and out if control, providers of bad service, too, will crumble. Quality has to remain the forefront of all employees' thoughts and actions."

Table 7: BATS

Great Service	Poor Service
• The shelter was large enough to hold at least 12 people • The employees walking the line of 200 people were friendly and professional • The bus transportation representative was professional	• The train service operated a defective announcing system • The train transportation officials had no employees to help during the malfunction • The airline had no control of the excessive lines, and displayed no empathy

BATS continued. "We have discussed quality customer service in terms of our experiences at different business establishments. Quality customer service has to be mixed with diversity."

"Effective management of diversity can increase an organization's productivity through ...increased problem-solving ability"(Greer, C.R., p. 46, "Human Resource Management, A Managerial Approach"). Diverse groups of thinkers are able to produce increased creativity.

This creativity turns into increased productivity and profits, and improved internal and external customer service. Increasing global and local competition is causing organizations to fight for survival. Companies supporting employees' ideas and skills are pulling ahead in the business community. An unsatisfied employee can cost an organization in regards to money, low productivity, high turnover, absenteeism, and reputation.

Diversity within an organization will allow it to move into new markets, improve employee relations, plus improve communications between employees and business units. The diversity of thoughts and information are tools that assist teams and organizations with the ability to thrive in the business world. Diversity is not hiring those who are different and then forcing them to behave the same way. Diversity pools ideas and people for a better business plan. In the end internal and external customer service thrives for the good of the businesses and institutions.

Questions

1. How does quality customer relate to diversity?

2. What will an effective diversity program within an organization allow it to do in relationship to customer service?

3. Name the different customers bases in this chapter?

4. How do companies' visions relate to quality customer service?

Notes

Notes

Quote

"Leadership is action not position."

Donald H. McGannon

(Chambliss, et al., p. 35)

Chapter 8

The Wrap-up

Focusing on the creation, implementation, and promoting of a strategic quality customer service education program is important to success. Customer service is a part of the communications process for the internal, as well as the external customer. What are communications and promotions in relationship to customer service? In order to understand how business communication works, it is necessary to define the term communications.

Communication in itself is a skill and an art form. Communication is as much a matter of relationships as it is about transmitting facts. Communication occurs between two or more people to relay a message. According to Russell S. Winer, "the sender is the source of the information. In business, the sender is the producer and the receiver is the customer or consumer. According to Russell S. Winer, "personal communication could be direct face to face interaction between customer and organization" (2004, p. 227). A positive out come is what the sender is hoping for, from the face-to-face contact. In the business industry, non-personal contacts are called the communication mix; advertising, direct marketing, personal selling, sales promotion, publicity, and miscellaneous. Organizations involved in the communication mix must be clear and consistent with the message they are sending to the receivers, customers, and potential customers. One part of communication is concerned with effectively and efficiently providing information about the business and the products to chosen target groups.

As it stands quality customer service is an essential work skill. Employees have to be aware of their verbal and non-verbal communications. This is of particular importance for front-line employees and all telephone representatives. In order for businesses, for profit or non-profit, to remain viable they must maintain a constant customer base.

All levels of management should remain cognizant of their customer service quality at all times. Managements' outlook on a subject matter are reviewed and acted upon by employees faster than the managers' actions. Management has to be prepared to correctly recognize and realize their individual emotional reactions to the emotional reactions of others. Managers have to be able to control their emotions and use their emotions to make effective business decisions. The emotional intelligence skills must be consistently developed. This development is the understanding of inner emotions and being able to control/manage those emotions. Managers of emotional intelligence must be aware of others' feelings, and be able to work with and produce the desired responses in others.

Effective management has to be friendly but firm. Management cannot be afraid of confrontation nor can it promote confrontation. Effectual management teams have to institute and demand high performance standards and positively promote such standards through emotional intelligence. Customer service standards are apart of this standard of high measure. Management can remain abreast of service levels through surveys plus by completing a review of a business' strengths, weaknesses, opportunities, and threats, SWOT.

Let's further define the internal customer? The internal customer is a co-worker within the same organization. This co-worker may work in the same building, work in a different building, or may work and reside in another state, or country. The internal customer can be a customer as well as supplier within the organization. This customer is anyone that you may rely on to get a portion of a job completed. In turn you may be the internal customer to the person you rely upon if that person depends on you to complete a portion of an assignment of job function. Successful organizations place a key focus on the internal customer.

As Fornal, (2002, June), aptly stated in the SHRM magazine, businesses focusing on its internal customers should "...sustain a team environment where employees not only recognize their dual role as customer and supplier but also are encouraged and rewarded to do so. Expectations are clear and constantly reinforced" ("Developing and Sustaining: Promote a Customer-Supplier Work Environment"). Internal customer service broadens itself to employee morale, external customer service, productivity, profitability, and all other areas of the business.

Who is the external customer? The external customer is one who requires the goods and/or services of an organization, but is not acting as an internal customer at the time of the goods and services exchange. This external customer will purchase goods and services providing income lending to profits and paying the bills.

All customer types react to verbal and nonverbal communications. Another way to restate communications is as the sending, receiving, and processing of verbal and non-verbal messages. In order to receive a message one has to listen to the message without preconceived notions. When a communicator listens to gain understanding, the communications process has the potential to move forward. This forward movement is enabled because the listener has an understanding of the situation and will be able to provide a stronger reply due to an increased understanding. Social psychologist, Albert Mehrabian, prepared a communication's model approximately 30 years ago which breaks down communication into three key areas.

- 7% of meaning is in the words that are spoken.
- 38% of meaning is paralinguistic (the way that the words are said).
- 55% of meaning is in facial expression

Understanding the difference between words and meaning is a vital capability for effective communications and relationships.

(Chapman, 2006, "Mehrabian Communication Research")

A visual of Mehrabian's findings can be seen in Chart 1.

Chart 1

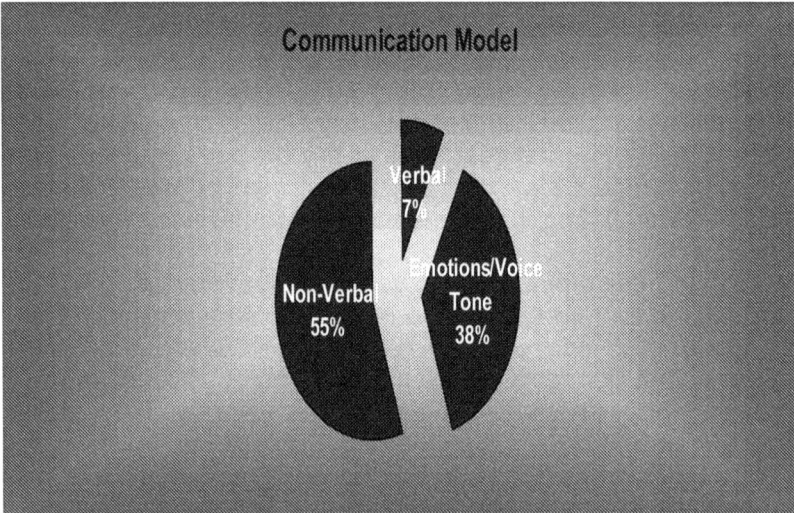

Verbal communications consists of words that convey numerous messages and produce an array of signals. All employees should receive education to speak with confidence, and diffuse highly concerned customers. Through the spoken word come volume, pitch, tone, emphasis, rate, pronunciation, dialect, and voice quality.

- Volume

The volume of the voice is important. A loud voice may indicate domination. Too slow of a voice may denote intimidation.

- Pitch

The pitch, height of the message, provides clarity to a message's meaning. For example. A high pitch means one may be excited, or upset.

- Tone

The tone helps to shape the message. The message may be delight, willpower, irritation, or indecision.

- Emphasis

Emphasis refers to the word or phrase the speaker focuses on when speaking.

- Rate

Rate is the speed at which we speak.

- Pronunciation

Pronunciation is the way words and phrases are spoken. Pronunciations will change according to the region of a country and between countries. When speaking, enunciate clearly.

- Dialect

Dialects may be specific to a select group of people. Examples of dialects are drawls, coal speak, Mid-western, New York, twangs, and numerous others.

▪ Voice quality	Phonetic labels exist for voice types. Some examples are "slow," "falsetto," and "whispery." These are just a few examples. Voice quality is important for speakers.

Words are used in many ways. When communicating via the phone with customers always sit straight. Sitting straight enables a clear and audible voice tone. While serving customers it is better to refrain from using, unless in a specified setting, complex words, euphemisms, jargon, profanity, plus slang and Ebonics. Let's look at these word types.

▪ Complex words	Complex words are those less known, or understood by the general learner. Employing simple and common words when possible will not upset readers' intellect. Simple terms add clarity.
• Euphemisms	Writers and speakers use euphemisms to replace strong and possibly offensive words with neutral and more positive sounding words.
• Jargon	Jargon is language particular to a trade, specialty, or business. For example, the language used by educators to discuss their work is different than the language used by engineers to discuss work.
• Profanity	Swear words should not be used when speaking with customers.

- Slang and Ebonics   Slang and Ebonics are non general usage of words, the creation of words, and the adoption of words from a different language.

Front-line employees are very important to an organization's bottom line. In today's economy of doing more with less, the front-line employees have to be educated to handle more difficult situations than ever before. These people will have to be educated to increase or maintain a pre-determined quality level, reduce costs, and increase moral. These employees should mentally ask themselves the following questions.

- Does my voice tone conflict with the words I am using?
- Am I communicating in an unclear or vague manner?
- How am I phrasing my messages?

The front-line representatives have to always deliver quality customer service with a smile. The quality service starts with the opening of the conversation, to professionally handling customers' expectations and perceptions, through to the close of the conversation. In addition to the front-line representatives' behaviors, the telephone representatives' behaviors can have a significant impact on business. The goal is for the impact to be positive.

Telephone representatives should receive education in proper telephone contact procedures. With appropriate pre-planning, the telephone representatives provide effective lines of communications for the organization. Telephone calls establish direct contact with customers so the representatives may gather the necessary information required to work through appropriate solutions to the customers' inquiries.

One shortcoming of telephone calls is the representatives must rely on the customers' voices to get the complete messages. Devoid of visual contacts, neither telephone representatives nor customers are able to depend on body language.

Businesses must understand their employees' needs, customers' needs, and have a strategic quality customer service education plan in place. Before implementing this education plan, businesses should perform a review of their strengths, weaknesses, opportunities, and threats analysis, SWOT.

SWOT is an outstanding tool for auditing organizations and their environmental conditions. The SWOT analysis gauges business units, proposals, and ideas. It does not measure the market. "A scan of the internal and external environment is an important part of the strategic planning process" (QuickMBA, 2004, "Strategic Management"). "Because it concentrates on the issues that potentially have the most impact, the SWOT analysis is useful when a very limited amount of time is available to address a complex strategic situation" (NetMBA, 2005, "SWOT Analysis"). In order to be in the winner's circle, organizations must be able to develop and implement strong strategy.

Businesses must deliver nonverbal communications in their training packages, also. Nonverbal messages are conveyed without words through facial expressions, posture, clothing, gestures, and other nonverbal messages. Nonverbal aspects surface from the orators' attitudes, self-images, self-confidence, and enthusiasm. This silent communications largely predicts the ways audiences respond to speakers. Listeners may learn more about what others may be saying by remaining aware of their nonverbal behaviors. Each culture will have different nonverbal techniques. Different cultures' speaking techniques will be dissimilar within the same country.

Businesses have to remain aware of their competitors' products and the quality of the products. As marketers of products and services, businesses must be aware of what customers are thinking about their competitors. Perception is more important than the actual when it comes to retailing customer service tangibles or non-tangibles, market share, and profits. Organizations will need to consistently maintain a matrix to compare how they rate against their competitors. The matrixes should be maintained for key product lines, whether tangible or intangible. In addition to being aware of the competitors' products and the quality of the products, businesses should have an understanding of their competitors' product service features.

What are product service features? These features add to quality customer service plus help to maintain a happy and returning customer base. Moreover, great service features increase businesses chances of a positive word of mouth business flow, referrals. When offered appropriately, the service features could become the staple for a business. Let's review some service features for banks, educational institutions, grocery operations, retailers, restaurants, medical facilities, and the transportation industry.

Banks/ Financial Industry	Product service features could be the number of services offered to customers, the amount of customer service representatives within the branches available to help customers, how fast the toll-free numbers are answered, or the number of free automated cash machines available.
Educational Institutions	Product service features could be the functionality for **all** student types to register on-line. The pleasantness, and knowledge of the numerous office staffs enhance the service features. Moreover, post-secondary service features could be the operating hours of their operations centers, meaning the hours are convenient for evening and week-end students, as well as the other students.

Grocery Operations	Product service features could be the width of the aisles. Whether or not the store has a pharmacy is another factor. The variety of items the store carries is even another service feature.
Retailers	Retailers have a number of key service features such as hours of operations, friendliness of the staff, the number of sales clerks available to assist customers, and the quality of the merchandise in relation to the price of the merchandise.
Restaurant Establishments	Restaurants must have great product service features to keep their customers returning. They should be clean and free of unpleasant odors. Restaurants should have friendly staffs who are familiar with the restaurant.
Medical Facilities/ Institutions	The product service features are many in this business. Drug representatives must be knowledgeable to service the different doctors' offices. Doctors' offices must be clean, and operating efficiently and effectively. These offices need friendly and knowledgeable staffs, also. In case of errors, drug companies' representatives have to be empathetic to the needs of it customers and listening audiences.

Transportation Industry	Whether the mode of transportation is by ground, air, or water, this industry should have friendly, knowledgeable, and educated staff members. The ability to get customers to their perspectives destinations on time is an important product service feature.

The packaging and display of product service features enhance businesses' services. All businesses must have something that is their staple to keep customers returning.

Another method competitors may employ to rise above in the customer service arena is to differentiate themselves from other businesses by using eye-catching tag lines. When customers enter competitors' operations, the difference should be clear as to which business continues to stand high above the competition. Businesses should maintain a vigilant eye on their competitors in order to increase their market share, sales, and higher quality customer perception in this industry. Businesses should keep in mind that their competitor targets must be watched consistently. Thus these operations should not only focus on their product service features, but focus on the product service features of the competition. Files of information should be maintained and reviewed when needed. This file maintenance will help to ensure the competition does not move ahead in the customer service arena.

Businesses with outstanding customer service differentiate between core values and practices. The employees are the people representing the core values and delivering the organizations' practices. Organizations' values and practices are parts of their brands. According to Eric Krell in the cover story of the October 2006 of HR Magazine, "...making sure they [employees] understand and can deliver the brand to customers is vital – especially for companies within the service industry, where the relationship between employees, and customers essentially is the product the company sells," (p.50).

Examples of companies with outstanding customer service are Commerce Bank, Wal-Mart, Home Depot, and Wawa's. The core values are not modified; however, the practices will be well thought through and tweaked. For example, Commerce Bank has a tab on its web-site for Customer Service. This is important to the customer. There is a toll-free number listed for customers to call with concerns. The information on the screen is noted in a font that is easy to read for all generations.

Wal-Mart reviewed customers' habits and determined that downloading is important to customers. According to the February 6, 2007 late edition of the New York Times, "Wal-Mart has formed a partnership with top Hollywood studios to sell digital movies and television shows on its web-site. Not only is it the first traditional retailer to do that, but its penchant for low prices could drive down the cost of a digital download." ("Movies from Walmart.com," p. C2).

Home Depot shows customers are first, too. The Financial Times' USA second edition published the following information written by Andrew Ward.

> ...when visitors entered the building for the company's annual analyst and investor conference yesterday, all evidence of Mr. Nardelli had disappeared. The space where the newspaper articles once hung was now occupied by pictures of ordinary employees and an organizational [sic] chart showing Home Depot as an inverted pyramid with customers at the top and the chief executive at the bottom.
> (2007, p. 21)

Quoting David Phillips, January 2002, Wawa's core values are "Value People, Delight Customers, Embrace Change, Do the Right Thing," ("With a dedication to...," *The way of Wawa*. p. 22)

One of the ways Wawa placed customers first is by instituting a coffee station with multiple flavors of coffee and cream. The stores have coffee hosts. These hosts ensure the self-service coffee stations remain filled and clean. The hosts talk with customers throughout the day.

Businesses should have a project plan for continual information sharing and innovation at all levels. Additionally, the leadership of a department has to be prepared to ensure the department does not run into cultural clashes, and cultural pitfalls. Quality customer service is undeniably one of the most essential skills needed within an organization. Customer service can either make or break a company. It is important for an organization to deliver and understand exactly what its customers need. " The quality of the product[s] and the service[s] will be remembered long after the price[s]... [are] forgotten... Make absolutely sure that your [products and] sales are backed up with excellent service" (Donleavy, 2000. Might is Right).

Businesses and governmental institutions that require standardization and sound quality should consider seeking ISO certification. With ISO comes a quality system that includes documented processes and procedures, policies, and training. Businesses incorporating ISO will have flow charts, user instructions, well written test scripts, written inspection processes, organizational charts, job/position descriptions, constant improvement processes, and customer satisfaction measures.

Organizational leaders should provide continual communications globally by employing an educational specialist and partnering with human resources. A key objective is to ensure employees are educated in regards to quality customer service and satisfaction. Again, customer service is not one specified item. It is a distinctive mixture of talent, practices, and methods. Customer service requires education, and consistent refocus. Let us all focus on the customers to ensure a strong rekindling of the art of service to customers. Review your customer service skills. What skill(s) can you enhance? Develop a 21 day action plan to enhance the skill(s) you have decided upon. Enhancing your chosen skill(s) will be about a daily resolve to continually improve.

21 Day Time and Action Plan

After determining which customer service skill(s) to enhance, document the skill(s).

Skill 1: _____

Skill 2: _____

Skill 3: _____

Skill 4: _____

Make a list of all the obstacles that may interfere with you enhancing your customer service skills.

Obstacles for Skill 1:

_____
_____
_____
_____
_____
_____
_____

Obstacles for Skill 2:

_____
_____
_____
_____
_____
_____

Obstacles for Skill 3:

_____
_____
_____
_____
_____
_____
_____

Obstacles for Skill 4:

_____
_____
_____
_____
_____
_____
_____

Make a list of how you will overcome the obstacles you anticipate
will interfere with enhancing your noted customer service skills.

Opportunities for Overcoming Obstacles for Skill 1:

_____
_____
_____
_____
_____
_____
_____

Opportunities for Overcoming Obstacles for Skill 2:

_____
_____
_____
_____
_____

Opportunities for Overcoming Obstacles for Skill 3:

_____
_____
_____
_____
_____
_____
_____

Opportunities for Overcoming Obstacles for Skill 4:

_____
_____
_____
_____
_____
_____

The next step is to make a list of how you will measure the results for each customer service skill you are working to enhance.

Measurement for Skill 1:

_____
_____
_____
_____
_____
_____

Measurement for Skill 2:

_____
_____
_____
_____
_____
_____
_____
_____
_____

Measurement for Skill 3:

_____
_____
_____
_____
_____
_____
_____
_____

Measurement for Skill 4:

_____
_____
_____
_____
_____
_____
_____
_____
_____

It is now time to begin documenting your daily results. You will need to chart the things you did to accomplish your goal(s) for enhancing customer service skills. This chart should be maintained daily. Remember, this chart is the location of your daily written actions. Move your thoughts and plans into actions.

Day 1

_____

_____

_____

_____

Day 2

_____

_____

_____

_____

Day 3

_____

_____

_____

Day 4

_____

_____

_____

_____

Day 5

_____

_____

_____

_____

Day 6

_____

_____

_____

_____

Day 7

_____

_____

_____

_____

Day 8

_____

_____

_____

_____

Day 9

_____

_____

_____

_____

Day 10

_____

_____

_____

Day 11

_____

_____

_____

_____

Day 12

_____
_____
_____
_____

Day 13

_____
_____
_____
_____

Day 14

_____
_____
_____
_____

Day 15

_____
_____
_____

Day 16

_____
_____
_____
_____

Day 17

_____
_____
_____
_____

Day 18

_____
_____
_____
_____

Day 19

_____
_____
_____
_____

Day 20

_____
_____
_____
_____

Day 21

_____
_____
_____
_____

How have your skills improved over the past 21 days.

_____

_____
_____
_____
_____
_____
_____
_____
_____
_____
_____
_____
_____
_____
_____
_____
_____
_____
_____
_____
_____
_____
_____

What could you have done to enhance your performance over the past 21 days?

_____
_____
_____
_____
_____
_____
_____

Questions

1. Document a SWOT using information in this chapter?

2. Define verbal and nonverbal communications?

3. Name the key aspects of front-line representatives and telephone representatives?

4. Develop a customer service guideline employing the key points in this book?

Notes

Notes

Notes

Chart of Characters

BATS   BATS represents the transportation industry. He is the meeting leader, and the main story teller.

Meaty   Meaty represents the grocery industry. He goes out to seek quality customer service in the grocery business.

Medic   Medic represents the medical industry. He goes out to seek quality customer service in the medical industry.

Peachie   Peachie represents the restaurant business. He goes out to seek quality customer service in the restaurant business.

Shopper   Shopper represents the retail industry. He goes out to seek quality customer service in the retail industry.

Stu   Stu represents educational institutions. He goes out to seek quality customer service in the educational arena.

References

Certo, S.C. (2000). Supervision, Concepts and Skill Building (3rd ed.).
USA: McGraw-Hill Higher Education.

Chambliss, A., Meisel, W., Wolf, M. (1991). Light One Candle, Quotes For
Hope And Action. White Plains, NY: Peter Pauper Press.

Goleman, D. (1995). Emotional Intelligence. New York: Bantam.

Greer, C.R. (2001). Strategic Human Resource Management, A Managerial
Approach. (2nd ed.). New Jersey: Prentice-Hall, Inc.

Krell E. (2006, October). "By including employees in branding...." *HR
Magazine*, 51, 50.

Nahavandi, A. (2003). The Art and Science of Leadership (3rd ed.). Upper
Saddle River, NJ: Prentice-Hall.

New York Times. (2007, February 6). Movies from Walmart.com. New
York Times [Late Edition], p C2.

Phillips, D. (2002, January). "With a dedication to quality and customer
service, diary celebrates a century of success." *The Way of Wawa*,
103, 22-26.

Podskoff, P.M., Mackenzie, S.P., Paine, J.B., Bachrach, D.G. (2000).
Organizational citizenship behaviors: a critical review of the theoretical
and empirical literature and suggestions for the future research.
Journal of Management, 26, pp. 513-563.

Schroeder, R.G. (2004). Operations Management (2nd ed.).

USA: McGraw-Hill Irwin.

Ward, A. (2007, March1, 2007). No news is good news in Home

Depot change. Financial Times [USA 2nd ed.]. p 21.

Webster's Ninth New Collegiate Dictionary. (1989). A Merriam-Webster Inc.

(9th ed.). Springfield, Massachusetts: USA.

Winer, R. S. (2004). Marketing Management (2nd ed.) Upper Saddle River,

New Jersey: Pearson Prentice Hall.

Web-sites

Bill Clinton Quotes. (n.d.). Think Exist.com Retrieved March 4, 2007, from

http://www.thinkexist.com/English/Author/x/Author_4554_1.htm

Chapman, A. (2006). Mehrabian Communication Research. Retrieved

March 4, 2007, from

http://www.businessballs.com/mehrabiancommunications.htm

Donleavy, N. (2000). Might is right. Retrieved November 25, 2005, from

http://www.ivenus.com/careers/features/WW-FullLength2-Wk27.asp

Fornol, P. P. (2002, June). "Developing and sustaining a high

performance organizational culture: Promote a customer-supplier

work environment." SHRM Information Center. Retrieved February 18,

2007, from

http://www.shrm.org/hrresources/whitepaperspublished/CMS000287

.asp

NetMBA. (2005). SWOT analysis. Retrieved February 18, 2006, from

http://www.netmba.com/strategy/swot/

PPP Retirement Plans. (n.d.). Creative Visualization for Positive Thinking.

Retrieved February 28, 2006, from

http://www.pppretirementplans.com/Creativevisualization.html

QuickMBA. (2004). *Strategic management*. Retrieved February 18, 2006,

from http://www.quickmba.com/strategy/swot/

Radeneau, S. W. (May 18,). The boiling frog. Retrieved February 5,

    2006, from http://www.sacredlands.org/boiling.htm

Radeneau, S. W. (May 18). The boiling frog; signs of distress:5000-

    3000 B.C.E. Retrieved February 5, 2006, from

    http://www.sacredlands.org/boiling.htm

Radeneau, S. W. (May 18). The boiling frog; signs of distress:3000-1400

    B.C.E. Retrieved February 5, 2006, from

    http://www.sacredlands.org/boiling.htm

Radeneau, S. W. (May 18). The boiling frog; signs of distress:1400-0

    B.C.E. Retrieved February 5, 2006, from

    http://www.sacredlands.org/boiling.htm

Radeneau, S. W. (May 18). The boiling frog; signs of distress:1200-1700.

    Retrieved February 5, 2006, from

    http://www.sacredlands.org/boiling.htm

Radeneau, S. W. (May 18). The boiling frog; signs of distress:1700-

    1900. Retrieved February 5, 2006, from

    http://www.sacredlands.org/boiling.htm

Radeneau, S. W. (May 18). The boiling frog; signs of distress:1900-60.

    Retrieved February 5, 2006, from

    http://www.sacredlands.org/boiling.htm

Radeneau, S. W. (May 18). The boiling frog; signs of distress:1960-96

    B.C.E. Retrieved February 5, 2006, from

    http://www.sacredlands.org/boiling.htm

Radeneau, S. W. (May 18). The boiling frog; signs of distress:1960

    to the present. Retrieved February 5, 2006, from

    http://www.sacredlands.org/boiling.htm

Williams, A. L. (2007). Malcom X College; Message from the Director.

    Retrieved February 26, 2007, from

    http://malcolmx.ccc.edu/aas/mortuaryScience/director.asp

Music

The W.E.S. Group. (2002). HET-HURA JAZZ

The Will Smith Quartet. (1989). HET-HURA Productions

Quote

"We have to improve life, not just for those who have the most skills and those who know how to manipulate the system. But also for and with those who often have so much to give but never get the opportunity."

Dorothy Height
(Chambliss, et al., p. 19)

Quote

"If you let ole' man can't move in, he will never move out."

Agnes Hill Williams, grandmother

(Daughter: James Hill & Laura Humble Hill, Stewart County, GA)

Epilogue

Transitioning to I Can from I Can't

The Story of Sherry

Transitioning to I Can from I Can't is an account of categorical life changing narratives designed to provide readers with another set of lenses for which to peer. The reader will be able to see situations appearing hopeless and negative evolve into mere limited time-frame circumstances. This enlightenment will shine through detailed stepped movements of individuals learning to transition from what appears to be hopeless conditions towards hope, and futures enlightened through preparation. One account is, *the Story of Sherry*.

Sherry is one such character who was born into a situation of daily beatings and mental degradation. Her mother, Elmetrice, a professional in the medical field, succumbed to the lure of drugs and alcohol before Sherry's birth.

As a very young child Sherry remembers the heart wrenching feeling of sheer fear every time she was in Elmetrice's presence. Unable to look into Elmetrice's eyes due to a history of consistently being slapped across the face with shoes, belts, electrical cords or whatever she could get her hands on, Sherry walked around the house with her head down.

Even though Sherry excelled in her school studies, and was dressed in nice clothing daily, she could not escape the label of being the "crazy lady's daughter". She could not flee the frequently asked questions, "Why do you have bandages on your legs every day?" "What is that odor?" "Why are you so skinny?" "What is wrong with your mother?" "Ain't she crazy?"

Sherry endured physical abuse, mental abuse, and loneliness, until one particular day, life's changing hand moved altering the course of her turbulent journey.

Quote

"If the ox is in the ditch get him out."

Agnes Hill Williams, grandmother

(Daughter: James Hill & Laura Humble Hill, Stewart County, GA)

SEMINAR SERIES LIST

Rekindling the Art of Service to Customers

For interest in the seminar series, please send an email to
qualitysolutions@verizon.net,
Or write to:
Quality Solutions by S. L. Burton
P.O. Box 7457
Wilmington, DE 19803

- *Rekindling the Art of Service to Customers in Education*

- *Rekindling the Art of Service to Customers in Call Centers*

- *Rekindling the Art of Service to Customers in Front-line Management*

- *Rekindling the Art of Service to Customers in Middle Management*

- *Rekindling the Art of Service to Customers in Senior Management*

- *Rekindling the Art of Service to Customers in Retail*

- *Rekindling the Art of Service to Customers in the Medical Industry*

- *Rekindling the Art of Service to Customers in the Grocery Business*

- *Rekindling the Art of Service to Customers in the Restaurant Business*

- *Rekindling the Art of Service to Customers in Banking*

- *Rekindling the Art of Service to Customers in the Transportation Industry*

ABOUT THE AUTHOR

Sharon L. Burton has an earned dual MBA in Human Resources, and International Business and Operations Management from American InterContinental University, in Hoffman Estates, Illinois. She holds a BS in Criminology from Florida State University, in Tallahassee, Florida. She holds several diplomas from the American Institute of Banking in Dover, Delaware. Additionally, she is a Toastmaster.

Sharon is a native of Georgia. She attended various schools: Dawson, GA; Moultrie, GA; Wilmington, DE; Donalsonville, GA; and Albany, GA.

She is the proud mother of one daughter, Yoshino N. Woodard, who has an earned MS in Industrial Engineering.

Sharon has managed within several Fortune 500 companies, and created ground-up training and development departments, created quality assurance and compliance departments, as well as handled duties as a HR Generalist Business Liaison. She has created and facilitated training in the areas of: Payroll Administration, Policies and Procedures, Customer Service, Communications/ Public Speaking, Mentoring Programs, Diversity, Train-the-Trainer, Credit and Collections, Project Management, and Operations Management.

Currently Sharon is an Administrator at Community College of Philadelphia.

She is available for speaking engagements, and seminars. For additional information about Sharon visit www.slburton.com or write:

Quality Solutions by S.L. Burton LLC
P.O. Box 7457
Wilmington, DE 19803

Quote

"Weight is the one that broke the wagon down. I am going to wait on the Lord and that is it."

Agnes Hill Williams, grandmother
(Daughter: James Hill & Laura Humble Hill, Stewart County, GA)

Notes

Notes

Notes

Notes

Notes

Notes

"Quality Customer Service is a journey.
It is not a destination."

Sharon L. Burton

ISBN-13   978-0-6151-4897-7

www.ingramcontent.com/pod-product-compliance
Lightning Source LLC
Chambersburg PA
CBHW022057210326
41519CB00054B/588